PRAISE FOR DARRELL MILLER AND *THE 16TH MINUTE OF FAME*

"Darrell is a great friend and one of the best entertainment attorney's there is."

—Daymond John, Founder/CEO of FUBU, Author, Co-host of ABCs *Shark Tank*

"The Bible rightly declares that in the multitude of counsel there is safety. Darrell Miller's insightful advice and extensive experience has been the impetus for a wisdom unrivaled for my entertainment initiatives. His book, *The 16th Minute of Fame* should prove invaluable for any reader who has to manage what they do and who they are becoming. A must read!"

—T.D. Jakes, Sr., Bishop, CEO of TDJ Enterprises and *New York Times* Bestselling Author

"Darrell is one of the smartest guys I know in the entertainment business I've had the pleasure of working with. Even better, I am fortunate to be able to call him my friend. In the end, true success in your career is when you triumph over your *16th Minute of Fame*."

—Chris "Ludacris" Bridges, Music Mogul & Actor

"Darrell Miller is one of Hollywood's most celebrated entertainment attorneys. In his over 20 years in the business, Darrell has seen countless people achieve fame. He's also seen them disappear—because they didn't prepare to extend their hard-won success to *The 16th Minute of Fame* and beyond. No matter what level of fame you reach—local, national or international—Darrell's "Seven Streams of Income" will prepare you to keep your success going."

—Donna Brazile, Political Strategist, Professor, Author & Syndicated Columnist

"When I decided to take my career to the next level and become more than just talent in front of the camera, I turned to my friend and adviser, Darrell Miller. He asks the important questions most people have never thought to ask. I encourage you to read *The 16th Minute of Fame* to learn the secrets of how to sustain your success."

—Shaun Robinson, *Access Hollywood*

"*The 16th Minute of Fame* is an insightful look into the key principles that sustain personal success for the long run and prevents the tragedy of 'making it' and then losing it. Whether you're pursuing a dream or have already achieved everything you've ever hoped for, read this book and get ready to live life to the fullest."

—Charles Lee, CEO of Ideation and
Author of *Good Idea: Now What?*

"Thank you Darrell Miller for these insights, gems and nuggets of brilliance. You have put your heart, money and soul into this important masterwork. I was not only informed and inspired, but empowered by your impressive research, commitment, words and ideas on this prickly subject of "fame," particularly in the Black community. You have the answers and they are timely and needed. All those charged with the responsibility of stardom and leading will learn valuable lessons by internalizing and acting on the rigorously thought-out steps and conclusions you've laid out in *The 16th Minute of Fame*. Bravo! We all now have something worth reading on this critical subject of processing, managing and leveraging whatever fame we may achieve in life. Thank you so much for this powerful gift."

—George C. Fraser, Author of *Success Runs In Our Race*
and Chairman, Fraser Net, Inc.

"This is a must read for anyone in the entertainment —
especially actors!"

—Bill Duke, Actor and Founder/CEO of Duke Media

"This book absolutely should be on the bookshelf of every
professional who works with celebrities or aspires to work
with high-profile talent in the sports and entertainment
industries. Darrell's depth of experience as an advisor
to the "Stars" gives him such a unique and relevant
perspective on the dangers that ensnare so many of our
creative talent who are lucky enough to taste—if only
for 15 minutes—fame and fortune, but who then crash
hard, having never made a plan for the life that comes
afterwards. This failure to understand the true boom-and-
bust-cycle that almost all high-profile talent go through
in these unique professions can be devastating, and the
only way out of the cycle is through successful planning
and foresight. This book provides a clear path for building
a successful plan and should become a part of the core
curricula for those of us who work with and support
entertainers and athletes around the world."

—David P. White,
National Executive Director, SAG-AFTRA

"I've had the great pleasure of sharing numerous clients with Darrell Miller throughout the years. My nickname for Darrell is "The Counselor" because he is more than just a great attorney but a consigliere! He is forward thinking and always keeps his clients long term goals and dreams forefront in mind. Darrell has an uncanny ability to visualize the big picture and in doing so, he is able to strategize for and alongside with those individuals to ensure that they can achieve long lasting and meaningful success. Any person interested in moving beyond the typical channels and conventional avenues should read this book."

—Charles King, Partner / Motion Picture Agent
William Morris Endeavor

The
16TH MINUTE
OF FAME

The
16TH MINUTE OF FAME

Darrell D. Miller

DUNHAM
books

Disclaimer
This book is meant to provide motivation and a general business strategy
for building and sustaining success; it is not meant, and should not me
used, to substitute for, or to supersede, professional, financial, or legal
advice.
Any testimonials or endorsements in, or related to, this book do not
constitute a guarantee, warranty, or prediction regarding the outcome of
your legal matter.

Trade paperback ISBN: 978-1-939447-75-3
Ebook ISBN: 978-1-939447-76-0

Printed in the United States of America

DEDICATION

To my beautiful daughter, Amari, who, at three-years-old, is already working an iPad better than many adults, counting her coins, and dreaming of developing multiple streams of income. May your dreams come true! I love you—Dad.

CONTENTS

INTRODUCTION

"In the future, everyone will be world-famous for fifteen minutes."

Andy Warhol coined that prophetic line in 1968. But even he likely couldn't have imagined just how true his prediction would become.

Today, fame is prolific. More and more people are getting a taste of public success thanks to the new digital revolution dominated by YouTube, Facebook, Twitter, Instagram, and the Internet, not to mention the hundreds of television channels available around the clock. It's also come true as a result of the reality TV craze with shows like *American Idol, Survivor, The Apprentice, The Real Housewives* franchises, and *America's Next Top Model*. A regular Joe can become Joe the Plumber in an instant. The world is under a microscope. Athletes, business executives, and politicians are susceptible to twenty-four-seven, on-demand news cycles that print, broadcast, and tweet all the news, all the time.

Fame sure isn't what it used to be.

As an entertainment attorney, I've had a first row seat for years, watching people dive in and out of success as quickly as a flip of the light switch. More and more people are getting a taste of the limelight, but very few have bothered to learn how to keep it. But success shouldn't have to be a fleeting thing. For those who are wise, success can be built to last.

I wrote this book to inspire people to think differently about achieving success. There are plenty of books available that tell you how to get it, but few of them tell you how to keep it in the 21st Century. My focus is on how and why you can *stay* successful. As you climb the ladder on a community, statewide, or global level, my goal is to motivate you to stop, take time, and give real consideration to some of the issues you will inevitably deal with when you grab your fifteen minutes of fame. If you are intentional with your brushes with success, you can grow a momentary joy into a lifelong adventure.

When life is good and things are popping on all cylinders, you're at an important crossroads. The choices you make, along with the way you think about your success, are crucial. You can either make wise, intentional decisions that will result in having a "sixteenth" minute of fame and fortune, or you can make poor, uninformed decisions that will see it all vaporize after those initial heady minutes of success.

The truth is, most people get a shot at being famous, but most don't stay famous for long because they're not prepared for the success they seek. Sustainable success is about the sixteenth minute. People who only focus on the limelight frequently end up only being a flash in the pan.

Right now, there are endless examples of people who have had, or are currently experiencing, their fifteen minutes of fame. And while we all might first think of Hollywood celebrities as the "famous" ones, there's so much more to the term than that. High school and local college level coaches and athletes, as well as local musicians, politicians, church leaders, educators, physicians, and community activists can all attain a tremendous level of recognition or notoriety in their local communities. They are often identified as people to whom citizens look up to and admire for leadership and guidance. In their fifteen minutes of fame, these individuals have a unique opportunity to elevate themselves and their communities to a higher level by impacting everything around them, including the brand and name recognition of their towns, jobs, education, healthcare, and small businesses.

On the corporate level, there are also numerous opportunities for individuals to achieve their fifteen minutes of fame. The studio development executive is promoted to vice president, the entertainment law associate makes partner, or the talent agent assistant, who traditionally starts in the mail room, is elevated to being an agent. In most situations where your name is equated with something good, positive, and notable, the inevitable rewards and upward movement provide you with the chance to make decisions that will impact both you and others for the long-term.

Your fifteen minutes can happen early in life as it did for computer and technology masterminds like Steve Jobs, Bill Gates, and Mark Zuckerberg, who rose to worldwide fame and fortune while still in their early twenties. Or it can also come much later in life, as it did for Ray Kroc who founded the McDonald's hamburger chain at the age of fifty-two. Or like actor Samuel L. Jackson who, in his early forties, finally hit it big in Hollywood after nineteen years of small supporting roles and bit parts.

Fame or "fifteen minutes" can even happen multiple times as a person enters new fields and achieves even greater levels of recognition. But if we accept Andy Warhol's prophetic statement to be true—*it will happen to you.* And you need to be ready for it.

My own personal philosophy is that life is fundamentally good. I expect and believe that great things will to happen to me. If you too accept this premise, you can live out of the knowledge that good things are headed your way. At some point you are going to get an opportunity to achieve something great in your life that has the *potential* to elevate you in your community or your business to the next level.

You will have your fifteen minutes of fame. Working under this knowledge, why *not think outside that* "fifteen minute" box and plan ahead for your future moment of success? Why be unprepared for something that is inevitably going to be yours? Why fall into the trap of not being ready for the success that you seek?

Everything I do is in preparation for great moments to occur in my life. Yes, of course, bad things *do* happen. Yes, there will be unwelcome surprises or setbacks—they are an inevitable part of life. But too many people seem to accept and dwell on the bad things rather than hope for and anticipate the good things—the big breaks or the transformative events that can take their lives to new and exciting levels.

If you live life expecting good things to happen and are willing to *plan* for those good things, you will be more attuned to the challenges that will inevitably occur along the way and will not be defeated by them when they happen. You'll view obstacles as a natural part of your journey. On the contrary, if you don't anticipate any challenges at all, you increase your chances of being blind-sided and defeated by them when they do arrive. You could completely squander away your good fortune because you're unable or too uninformed to make the right decisions to extend your newfound success, fame, and fortune.

Wishing, wanting, and waiting just won't cut it. After

all, eighty percent of success in the entertainment industry comes from access and preparation.

Over the course of my career in entertainment, I have seen far too many talented people who are first generation wealthy, attaining "everything they've ever wished for" at their peak of glory, only to totally waste their golden moment due to lack of good preparation. They simply weren't ready to go beyond their early achievements and didn't know how to handle the fruits of their success.

I don't want to see that happen anymore. My singular goal in writing *The 16th Minute of Fame* is to help you reach your full potential. This means not squandering the success that is gifted to you, but instead extending it far beyond those first fifteen minutes of fame. I want you to be around to experience ongoing success in the long run—after the lights have dimmed, the applause has faded, and you've had your biggest moment in the sun. I want to equip you with the tools and wisdom to help you to continue to enjoy that success you so sweetly earned. There is so much more for you than a flash in the pan.

Doors are being opened for you. The question is: do you have the courage to walk through them?

Darrell D. Miller
Los Angeles, 2014

PREFACE
by Angela Bassett

When I was first introduced to Darrell Miller a little over ten years ago, I was already blessed with a wonderful stage, television, and film acting career propelled by my Oscar nomination for the movie, *What's Love Got to Do With It?*. I can't believe it's been twenty years! It was a dream come true to reach such a level of popularity and acclaim within the Hollywood movie industry, along with the support of the overwhelming number of new fans from all over the world. I was humbly grateful and appreciative of the great rewards that came along with the offers that were pouring in. But I considered acting to be my calling, not my career, and I left the everyday and business concerns to an excellent team of the usual professionals—an agent, manager, PR person, and legal representation. It was all going very well, but eventually I felt that I needed to bring in someone with a fresh, "outside the box" point of view to capitalize on the practical side of my growing creative and commercial success. I didn't want to go to the normal route of hiring the same traditional Hollywood lawyers. Instead, I wanted to find a way to put together a more forward-thinking team.

Once we were introduced, Darrell and I hit it off immediately and built a special bond based on our remarkably similar backgrounds. Although we were current residents of the glamorous Hollywood community, we had both experienced childhoods raised in small towns— Cincinnati, Ohio and St. Petersburg, Florida. Both of our heads, then, had been filled with dreams of performances, audiences, and applause. As someone who has walked the same road, Darrell has a unique business perspective that's born of compassion.

Working with Darrell has been incredible. His strength, his legal savvy, his ability to be supportive, and his ready availability for consultation have been impressive and inspiring. He is sincerely passionate and profoundly dedicated to helping his clients reach all of their goals.

Right from the start, Darrell presented an innovative (at the time) concept: being a celebrity was not what it used to be. Before, a successful actor could depend on revenue from one primary source in the entertainment industry to sustain a very lucrative career and a very comfortable lifestyle. That didn't work anymore. Darrell quickly demonstrated how his theory of creating multiple streams of revenue could work for me, explaining that the value of the assets that I had built through my art could go beyond what acting in Hollywood movies was providing at the time. Darrell helped me pull together a series of revenue streams that immediately began to expand my excitement, creativity, and contribution to the entertainment industry.

I have always been deeply thankful to be able to do what I love—and have loved since I first found acting when I was just a teenager. While I was in school, my mother, much like Darrell's family, always stressed education. I could respect that and I put my nose to the grindstone, determined to avoid skipping classes or goofing off no matter how tempting or persuasive my friends were. In high school though, I was more than just a student attending classes. I was also a member of the student government, drama club, choir, and cheerleading squad. Darrell would say that I was "building streams" even then!

After I graduated from Yale College and Yale University with my master's degree, there were three things on my list as I started out in the real world: I wanted to work consistently, I wanted to do good work, and I wanted to be paid fairly. Needless to say, I have been truly blessed and have been able to check off all three. I didn't become an actress for the money, but I'm grateful to have been rewarded with significant earnings. Because I believe that acting is my "calling," I've never felt the need to celebrate and waste the fees I'm paid. Actually, I'm quite conservative about my finances. I'll take chances with my career and accept challenging roles or a small obscure film—I gamble with that all the time—but not with my money!

In my experience, Darrell's ideas and concepts of how to navigate the sixteenth minute of fame by diversifying and investing in your assets and influence are absolutely invaluable. Nowadays, we all see talented kids coming out of school and directly into the limelight—whether it's on a stage, an office, a sports field, or a recording studio—who seem to take it for granted that living a fabulous star's life is going to last forever. Unfortunately, they soon find out the hard way that in reality fame, and the money that often comes with it, only last for a hot minute. I teach my kids that they need to learn to delay gratification—life isn't about getting everything you want exactly when you want it. Ironically, when I say, "No" and my kids have a great attitude about thinking of ways to earn what they are asking for, they usually end up getting whatever I've been refusing a lot sooner! Darrell promotes the same attitude in all of his clients and now, in his book, *The 16th Minute of Fame*, he is sharing his concepts and theories that can help anyone who's on a path to success whatever their passion, talent, or vision.

I have played many strong, fascinating, real-life women in African-American culture, including Tina Turner in *What's*

Love Got to Do with It, Katherine Jackson in *The Jacksons: An American Dream*, Rosa Parks in *The Rosa Parks Story*, Voletta Wallace in *Notorious*, Betty Shabazz in *Malcolm X* and *Panther*. Through their stories, and my own personal experiences, I have seen a great deal of life worth living despite mistakes, poor decisions, and tragedies around me. Darrell presents lessons each of us can take with us in some measure—large or small, as we build and maintain our careers.

Like Darrell, I believe it's vital that no one settle for average and that it's important to always bring your best and give it all you have—whether you fail or succeed. In pursuit of my personal multiple streams of revenue branching into other interests, we are currently in talks for my directorial movie debut. I really appreciate what directors do. I know it's a lot of responsibility and I have been working hard to learn that craft. My husband, Courtney B. Vance, and I wrote a book called, *Friends: A Love Story* based on our fifteen-year relationship. I have the honor to be named a UNICEF Goodwill Ambassador for the United States. Many people don't know that I'm also the voice of Michelle Obama on *The Simpsons*. In recent years, with Darrell's help, I set up a production company, Bassett Vance Productions, to develop content and to leverage me as a producer in Hollywood. Over the years, Darrell has also encouraged me to accept roles on both major studio and more obscure independent films to broaden my range, appeal, and influence to an even greater audience.

For many years I've been blessed with Darrell's wise career advice. Now his book, *The 16th Minute of Fame,* will give other artists, athletes, and entrepreneurs the courage and wisdom to step beyond their first "fifteen minutes" and extend their successful careers of today to secure their future!

Angela Bassett is an Emmy and Academy nominated, Image Award and Golden Globe winning American actress.

FOREWORD

by Blair Underwood

Back when I was still in high school, I was given some pivotal advice by a woman who had been in the business for a while; "if you're really serious about acting," she said, "then you need to hone every discipline you can." I think one of the most difficult challenges in show business is the challenge of longevity. How does one stay relevant, engaged, bankable, and simultaneously create a legacy? *The 16th Minute of Fame,* by my friend and lawyer, Darrell Miller, perfectly addresses these challenges and more.

I first met Darrell Miller socially through colleagues in the entertainment industry, several years ago. He has always had a unique perspective and insight into how to create significant revenue in show business that is completely relatable. I was greatly impacted by his ahead-of-the-curve messaging about expanding revenue and long-term plans beyond acting and, seven or eight years later, Darrell and I became working colleagues.

THE 16TH MINUTE OF FAME

At one point, he told me I am a perfect example of his key message for his seven streams of revenue theory. In fact, whenever I run into Darrell around town, before I say "hello," I often greet him with a running joke by calling out, "multiple streams of revenue!" as soon as he's in sight. There is always a good and productive dialogue that follows.

The movie *Krush Groove* was my first break. I had just moved to New York right out of college and I was just happy to have a job. Many years later, Darrell inspired me to explore a number of different disciplines in order to become a prolific entrepreneur and actor, including business and philanthropic ventures, speaking engagements, books, live stage productions, acting in small films or big films, and starring on television network dramas. For example, I've been developing a line of "Blair Underwood" suits with K&G, a division of Men's Wearhouse, that has led to a lucrative partnership that enables me to extend both my brand and my potential, and to establish a new stream of income into the retail market.

At this point in the game, the thing I'm most grateful for in my career is to be able to have success in the different mediums of television, film, and the stage.

I have been working in the film industry for twenty-eight years, and to be still standing and thriving in this business is a great feeling. Those years have taught me that if one project doesn't last, something else will soon present itself.

I am very careful as to the image I present that is perceived by the public. As an actor with multiple income streams to handle, I have moved beyond simply playing good guy/bad guy roles, and in keeping with Darrell's "Seven Streams of Income" principle, I have become more interested in getting into other business endeavors and entrepreneurial ventures stemming from my acting career.

I must credit Darrell with inspiring me to think about and to really refine my business/life strategy by creating multiple streams of revenue. In many ways, I am living Darrell's message and exponentially growing a number of streams of income. Our first deal together was a success and it was only natural that we would move forward to concentrate on finding other endorsements, advertisements, and multi-hyphenate projects that would continue to build my brand, along with discovering new ways to create revenue streams for the retailer. I often like to talk to young people who aspire to be in show business or any other business that they're passionately involved in. I am very grateful to have people in my life—*warriors*—who have supported me and who sometimes give me words of wisdom. Darrell Miller is one of those warriors. Whether I'm stepping into the publishing world, the stage, or in films or television, Darrell has been right there with me offering smart advice and strong, creative ideas.

In Langston Hughes' poem, "A Dream Deferred," he poses the question, "if a dream is deferred, does it dry up, like a raisin in the sun or does it fester like a sore, and then run...or does it explode?"

I still have a multitude of dreams yet to be realized, and the concepts Darrell shares in his book, *The 16th Minute of Fame* completely embody these goals and dreams. We live in a day and age with far-reaching technology. What you do today—what you put on film or on tape—what you write on a page or tweet to a friend—what products you endorse with your name—is in cyberspace in an indelible instant. It will be all over iPads, iTunes, and the Internet and it'll still be there long, long after you're gone. With Darrell Miller's advice and guidance in *The 16th Minute of Fame*, I am confident that I'll have no regrets.

Blair Underwood is a Grammy Award winning American actor who has been nominated for two Golden Globes and has won three Image Awards.

Chapter 1

RAGS TO RICHES TO RAGS

"Be sure to know the condition of your flocks, give careful attention to your herds, for riches do not endure forever, and a crown is not secure for all generations." —Proverbs 27: 23[1]

One of the hard luck stories most pervasive in today's society revolves around the fact that many people who achieve their life-changing fifteen minutes of fame inevitably crash and burn because they fail to sustain it. Unfortunately, after enjoying the fruits of those fifteen minutes, many people end up rapidly fading from the public eye and, even more often, losing the fortune that comes with it.

We have all heard of rags-to-riches stories. It's certainly no myth that many of our greatest achievers ascended from humble beginnings. We eagerly trace their roots from poverty and unfit families to stardom. And just as eagerly, we follow as these well-chronicled fairytales end with a celebrity's precipitous fall back down into the abyss of financial hardship later in life.

The hard reality is that more often than not people neglect to build on their sudden success and grow their first generation riches or "new money" into real long-term generational wealth. Whether they consume their wealth all by themselves or whether they're joined by so-called friends, family, fans, and admirers—what they've gained is lost all too quickly. No longer is it "rags to riches." Now it's "rags to riches to rags." Working for many years in the Hollywood entertainment industry, I've witnessed firsthand how a lethal mix of fast money, first generational wealth, and the appearance of fame can undo those who would otherwise flourish for the long-haul. For me, it's heartbreaking to watch worthy people waste away their futures, and so I became motivated to help change this reality.

I arrived in Los Angeles in the summer of 1989, to participate in the summer associate program at the LA office of a large Chicago law firm named Lord, Bissell & Brook. That summer, I was hired by their Chicago office, but I was allowed to split my time in the program spending half of it in Chicago headquarters and the other half in the satellite LA office. This was a dream come true for me. In those days, it was extremely rare for a Cincinnati native, who was educated on the east coast, to secure a job with a LA law firm right out of law school.

After graduating from Georgetown University Law Center, I was eager to begin my law career and immediately moved to Los Angeles on a permanent basis in 1990, to work at Lord Bissell & Brook's civil litigation department. However, shortly after I started at the firm, I expressed my interest in building a transactional entertainment law practice at the firm and the partners allowed me to pursue my dream in my spare time. The early '90s in LA was an exciting time, as Rupert Murdoch was in the process of launching Fox as the fourth broadcast network. Independent producers, film studios, and distribution companies were successfully experimenting with low-budget films that opened the door for many new filmmakers. A new technology called the Internet was buzzing as Americans began exploring on the Information Super Highway, which soon was projected to be offering five hundred channels for the distribution of programming and other forms of content. The combination of new delivery platforms, independent film production, and a new broadcast network that actually succeeded where so many others had failed, opened a world of opportunities for me. Ultimately, it validated my decision to pack up my life on the east coast and move to LA to start a new career.

As of 2014, I've spent more than twenty-three years working in the entertainment industry. In that time, I've been privy to many stories that showcase the bad decisions that are made every day by artists, athletes, and business executives who don't take the time to make good business and long-term life decisions. I've witnessed, with startling ease, how artists quickly make millions of dollars, then burn through it in just a few years, sadly assuming there will just be more at the end of the trail.

I remember arriving in LA and learning of the particularly depressing stories of two famous stars who died broke: the irreverent comedian Redd Foxx and the incomparable singer, dancer, and actor, Sammy Davis, Jr. Their stories had a huge impact on my understanding of the celebrity entertainment business and inspired me early on in my professional career to help artists, athletes, and other new-moneyed celebrities to look at fame and fortune differently.

Redd Foxx became a huge television star in the 1970's with his hit comedy series *Sanford and Son,* which was one of the most successful television shows of the decade. According to the Nielsen ratings, *Sanford and Son* made it to the top ten lists every year during its first five years on the air. However, the comic's battles with the IRS proved to have an even bigger impact. His IRS troubles were so bad at one point, it was widely reported that federal agents seized his house and assets including removing jewelry from his body.[2] According to *People* magazine, "Foxx reportedly once earned $4 million in a single year, but depleted his fortune with a lavish lifestyle, exacerbated by what he himself called 'very bad management.'"

In the 1950's and '60's, Sammy Davis Jr. was often recognized as one of the best-known and beloved entertainers alive. Davis' career spanned music recordings, concerts, TV, movies, and Broadway. He was an icon for the ages and a prominent member of the glamorous, bad boy "Rat Pack" along with Frank Sinatra, Dean Martin, Jerry Lewis, Peter Lawford, and Joey Bishop. Although Sammy was able to pull in a seven-figure salary—which was considered quite astronomical at the time—during the height of his career, he himself admitted to living an extremely extravagant, and often booze-filled lifestyle that far exceeded his impressive income. Due to his troubles with past-due taxes, much of his treasured memorabilia was auctioned off to pay the IRS after his death in 1990, which still left his widow Altovise with a reported $5 million dollar probate debt.

These larger-than-life, seemingly indestructible stars achieved great success only to lose it all by what appeared to be making poor decisions and bad choices that hurt their careers, their brands, their families, their communities, and their chances of maintaining their success. Had they only used more wisdom and discernment concerning their finances, their choices of representatives and the management of their brands, they could have substantially improved their chances of exiting life on top of the world and leaving their loved ones well-off for generations to come.

While the stories of Redd Foxx and Sammy Davis, Jr. opened my eyes in the beginning of my career, over the years, I have noticed a wide variety of stories and people who appear to be plagued by the same problem.

The most dramatic example of the "rags-to-riches-to-rags" phenomenon is the lottery winner. It's a common story: the winner has religiously played a lucky number for several years and suddenly a miracle happens—the number hits and the formerly poor or blue-collar worker is now a multi-millionaire, envisioning a wonderful life of endless luxury and leisure ahead. It's an understandable assumption that many people make, but in reality that scenario usually has a far different outcome.

One lottery winner spent the previous years of her life living an impoverished to modest existence laced with hopes of winning the jackpot. In all likelihood, over the course of those lean years, she never gave much thought to actually preparing herself for the day that she might, in fact, win the lottery. She focused her dreams on being an instant multi-millionaire, with the ability to buy anything her heart desired, indulge her every whim, and travel anywhere she wanted to go for the rest of her life. Because the future winner had modest beginnings, she did not fully understand what it meant to be a multi-millionaire and how to manage her windfall. It would never occur to her to research smart investments or to seek solid advice from knowledgeable family members or friends about the real responsibilities that come with being suddenly "rich" for the first time.

Once the winning numbers were confirmed, our "celebrity-for-a-day" winner was at first the center of a blaze of publicity involving local and national newspapers, Internet bloggers, TV talk shows, evening network news programs, and the twenty-four-hour cable news channels. Her friends and family were calling, shady people with questionable business deals were calling, the church was calling and, of course, the IRS was calling. The newly minted millionaire was overwhelmed by the demands that came with her fifteen minutes of fame. The "lucky" winner was simply not prepared for this bewildering new life, and she certainly hadn't given much thought to the most important aspects of her future that directly influenced her financial security for the rest of her life.

Instead, she announced her new plans with understandable euphoria: "I'm rich! I'm going to build my dream house. I'll buy that Mercedes 500 I've always wanted. I'll throw the party of all parties for my friends and take my family on a fabulous, all-expenses-paid holiday. I'll donate money to the church and my favorite charity, and hand out cash gifts to my favorite relatives who have always been there for me."

The lottery winner was more preoccupied with the outward symbols of consumption and display of wealth than she was in creating long-term opportunities for herself that would sustain her wealth-generating ability well into the future. She did not truly understand that the decisions she made while celebrating her luck in the spotlight would affect what happens in her future long after the lights are out. It's not surprising that a great majority of lottery winners eventually end up in bankruptcy court only a few years after winning the jackpot. The results of a 2010 study by researchers from Vanderbilt University, the University of Kentucky, and the University of Pittsburgh are even more troubling, suggesting that the bigger the win, the higher the chances are that a lottery winner will end up in bankruptcy.[3] Many of our most popular professional athletes and entertainers who achieve first generational fame and fortune are really not too different from these lottery winners. For instance, take a young boy who dreams of playing in the NBA one day. In pursuit of his hoop dreams, he practices diligently for several hours a day, lifts weights, watches his diet. The boy spends his spare time consumed with ESPN, *Sports Illustrated*, sports-related websites, video games, and viewing hours of tapes of all the great players. He fantasizes endlessly about what his life will be like once he's scouted and picked up by the pros.

Our society blatantly glorifies the athlete, and on his road to the big leagues our star player is courted by scouts and colleges and treated like a king. He's a star jock in high school and eventually earns a scholarship to a top, sports-dominated college. Once there, the talented athlete practices up to ten hours a day, typically placing his studies and his overall personal development on the backburner in the face of the demands of his sport. His focus has become all about excelling in basketball and, like many healthy young males, getting the girls. On the court, our player continues to excel. By the end of the season, he is a "March Madness" hero, and, finally, when the NBA draft is held, he gets his big break and signs a multi-million dollar contract to play in the NBA.

Despite outward appearances, all is not perfect here. The core problem is that this newly-minted professional athlete who has spent the greater part of the past twenty-two years preparing to be a basketball player on the court, has spent very little time, if any, learning what it actually means to achieve success and how to handle this new larger-than-life persona off the court. His new league, advisors, and coaches may send him to one or two crash course seminars on "how to invest your money" or "life off the court," but these courses rarely get his attention or have any real impact on his long-term thinking about how to maintain his fame and fortune. He hasn't been truly taught the importance of saving, investing money, or the basics of good financial planning. Like so many other high achievers who naively believe that their success will never end, the athletic hopeful willfully ignores the fact that the average NBA career spans less than five years. In a few rare exceptions, a career can be extended beyond that of the average player, such as the case of hall of fame star Robert Parish who played an astonishing 1,611 games over twenty-one seasons for the Golden State Warriors, Boston Celtics, Charlotte Hornets, and Chicago Bulls.

Our newly signed NBA star has not prepared himself for the possibility of a season or career-ending injury or illness. Oftentimes, in our fast moving, jock-admiring world, young men like our player—who have been treated like campus gods throughout their school years—have not been taught the importance of having a good moral character that is founded in integrity or what it really means to be a role model for millions of kids. In fact, in some cases, our greatest star athletes today reject the clean-cut image of a classic sports star and loudly claim that they are *not* role models at all.

The sports industry is loaded with examples of people who ultimately blew their fortunes because they were grounded in nothing but the superficial. Take a look at the facts:

- Seventy-eight percent of retired NFL players go bankrupt or experience financial hardship within two years after the end of their professional careers.[4]

- Up to sixty percent of retired NBA players end up in bankruptcy court or are broke within five years after they retire from the NBA.[5]

If you search the Internet for anything remotely close to "sports star files for bankruptcy," you're most likely to see a shocking list of familiar names who once commanded millions of dollars for their skills on the court, on the field, on the ice, or in the water—only to end up filing for bankruptcy once their careers were over. Mike Tyson is one of the most notorious examples of financial ruin in sports. He reportedly earned more than $300 million during his impressive boxing career, but was forced to file for bankruptcy. He's not alone though. He joins the ranks of stars like Johnny Unitas, Eric Dickerson, Antoine Walker, and Andre "Bad Moon" Rison.[6]

Imagine the difference that sound preparation and guidance could have made in the life of former NFL great Michael Vick who infamously filed for bankruptcy protection after being convicted of illegal dog fighting. Surprisingly, Vick's bankruptcy came only two years after he received a multi-million dollar player contract that included a $20 million signing bonus. Ultimately, Vick's conviction, along with his legal and other related bills, put him over $20 million in debt.[7] In another example, how is it that former NBA super star Latrell Sprewell, who played thirteen seasons in the league and rejected a $21 million contract extension from the Minnesota Timberwolves, could end up filing for bankruptcy protection? Sprewell earned tens of millions of dollars over the course of his career. His New York Knicks contract alone totaled $62 million.

Citing expensive divorces as a main culprit for his financial woes, former baseball giant Jose Canseco's home went into foreclosure. Baseball hero Lenny Dykstra also joined the troubled finances club when he listed a debt to various banks and law firms totaling over $30 million dollars, which forced him into bankruptcy.[5] Power golfer John Daly also fell into this group after four divorces and a staggering loss of as much as $50 million from gambling during his professional golf career.[8]

If you ask any athlete, they will tell you that many of their peers fall into financial hardship largely due to their out-sized competitive spirits. They compete with each other professionally on the field and that dynamic carries over to their personal lives. If your teammate buys a Rolex, then you just have to buy a more expensive brand. If your teammate buys a Porsche, then you absolutely must buy an even pricier, tricked out model. The need to compete can become dangerous if left unchecked, and can inevitably lead back to "a life of rags" for those who place all of their focus on fleeting enjoyment.

Artists and entertainers also tend to have their share of troubles when attempting to manage the trappings of sudden fame and fortune. The classic case of the "struggling actress" is an excellent example.

An actress has been hustling auditions and performing for years in regional theaters. She faithfully shows up to casting calls hoping for her first big break to become a Hollywood celebrity. She occasionally books bit parts in movies and television shows while struggling to pay her bills through a series of temp jobs as a receptionist or working as a waitress or a barista. Then, one day, it happens. Her agent calls with the news that she has been booked as a series regular on a hit television series. Overnight, her annual income increases significantly from $9,000 a year to $900,000 a year. In her mind, the good life has arrived and there is no turning back to the 99-Cent store. Instead of wisely saving some of her new ungraded salary and perhaps living modestly, our young actress immediately elevates her lifestyle to that of other more established stars around her. In her attempt to mirror their success and superstar style, the actress often succumbs to making any number of mistakes, including:

- Hitting Rodeo Drive in Beverly Hills for the hottest designer labels,
- Signing the lease for an expensive condo or house in the hippest part of town,
- Leasing a new luxury vehicle—or two!

- Signing with a major talent agency, a personal manager, an entertainment lawyer, a business manager, and a publicist as her team of representatives,
- Enrolling a "glam-squad" to handle her hair, make-up, and styling.

Our formerly unemployed and non-famous actress is now fully committed to the celebrity fantasy of being a "star," secure in the knowledge that she has "arrived." For a while, the actress' strategy pays off. She is featured in magazines and tabloids and perhaps even graces a cover or two. She makes appearances on the celebrity circuit of television and radio shows, and is a staple on Internet gossip sites. Fans by the thousands blog and tweet about her with rabid interest in her most insignificant move. For the moment, our girl is unquestionably a hot property as she revels in the fifteen minutes of fame that some industry insiders might call "hype."

It's ironic that at any given time, most actors in the professional Screen Actors Guild ("SAG") are back to square one within a disconcertingly short time of their original success. SAG regularly reports unemployment rates for its member in the range of eighty percent, with the twenty percent employed including minor roles and extra work. Less than one percent of working actors ever make it big.[9]

In addition, it's commonly understood in the industry that developing an idea, landing a pilot deal, and producing a successful television series is a very unpredictable long shot.

It's not surprising that life was looking rather wonderful for our actress until her once popular show slides in the ratings and is eventually cancelled by the network. Just like that, she finds herself back where she started, but she now has a lifestyle that requires her to earn $900,000 plus per year—and she's out of work. The actress soon finds herself in a most desperate situation with maxed out credit cards, a luxury car note, and an expensive apartment lease payment due every month. There's also an additional burden stemming from the emotional distress of dealing with the cancellation of her show and immediate unemployment. With all of those pressures to contend with, the young actress is faced with the harsh reality of the competition from a daily onslaught of new and more beautiful starlets arriving in Hollywood to take her place. She is back among the many unemployed actors in LA hustling from audition to audition, hoping for another hit. To illustrate my point, look through any entertainment magazine or surf the popular entertainment industry websites and gossip blogs and read the "Where Are They Now?" section, which is littered with the has-been faces of hits past.

A colleague once shared with me an amazing true story about an artist who received a $5 million signing bonus, along with a lucrative contract. Before the news of the deal had even been made public, the artist's celebratory first stop was a Bentley car dealership where he gleefully bought five Bentley automobiles at a whopping $450,000 per car. The artist was ecstatic that he had "hit the big time and had finally made it!" He had his fame and fortune, and he was not looking back. He went from driving a used, but perfectly functional car to planning to purchase a Bentley for every day of the work week. This was his way of confirming to himself that he had "arrived."

Fortunately, my colleague arranged for the artist's accountant to go down to the dealership and talk him out of jumping so quickly off the deep end and making such a reckless purchase. Although this example is rather extreme, impulsive decisions like this are made every day in my business. In fact, it's this kind of poor decision that ultimately results in a financial doomsday down the line.

One of the most infamous examples of the "rags-to-riches-to-rags" phenomenon is the hip-hop recording artist M.C. Hammer, who rose to super stardom with songs like "U Can't Touch This," "Too Legit to Quit," and "Let's Get It Started." In the late '80's and early '90's, Hammer's worldwide popularity seemed unending and, at one point in his career, he reportedly amassed a fortune exceeding $30 million. Now, I don't think Hammer ever thought, "I'm going to *make* $30 million, *spend* $35 million, and *end up* $5 million in the hole." He perhaps naively had an overwhelming desire to be a great performer and live like the other rich and famous people he now called his peers. Thirty million dollars is a lot of money—but it's relative. If you hang out with media moguls making $200 million, you might forget there's a huge discrepancy between your financial realities and then be tempted to live beyond your means.

Much of M.C. Hammer's financial problems seemed to have stemmed not only from poor financial literacy, but also from a desire to help a huge posse of friends and loved ones. Hammer spent his fortune at such an alarming rate. It was widely reported that he purchased a multi-million dollar home that was an open house to his posse. Hammer famously insisted on taking a busload of his extended family along for his performance tours. Since the record company enforced their agreement and shifted all of the tour expenses to the artist's column, Hammer was held responsible for the lion's share of everyone's accommodations, meals, and travel expenses. It doesn't take a financial wizard to know that Hammer's money rapidly evaporated, leaving only fumes behind, making his story of ruin a cautionary tale for anyone in the music business today.

In today's world, immediate gratification is a dominant force and we must come to realize a simple truth: *We have become a society of consumers rather than a society of savers and builders.*

The Federal Reserve reports that Americans carry $2.56 trillion in consumer debt, which is up twenty-two percent from 2000. For example, when someone gets a raise at work, they often make the choice to immediately upgrade their cost of living rather than saving the differential increase in salary. They don't think about preparing for the future or saving money for retirement. Any kind of windfall is a pass to go right to living in the moment. As a culture, we seem to be conditioned to not think much about life beyond any sudden good fortune. We want it and we want it now! The last subprime mortgage debacle, the bank failures, the rampant credit card debt, a declining yet pervasive SUV obsession, or a five-dollar a day coffee habit are all reflective of our state of affairs and exemplify the price we must now pay collectively for our lack of financial and business planning in the past. The National Endowment for Financial Education reports that about seventy percent of all people who unexpectedly get rich, end up broke within a few years.[10]

In spite of this sobering statistic, true financial and professional stability *can* be attained. It is not an impossible feat. Through discipline, hard work, sound advice, determination, and *focusing on sustaining success and not just achieving it*, many of the financial hardships that people find themselves in might be more easily minimized or avoided all together. If we begin to train ourselves to learn more about what it takes to sustain success rather than putting all of our eggs in the basket of endless laboring to become successful, more people would handle their golden opportunities differently. It's essential to understand that fame and fortune should always be taken seriously to avoid becoming the next rags-to riches-to-rags story.

Chapter 2

THE ROOTS OF FAME: PREPARATION FOR SUCCESS STARTS EARLY

"For me, winning isn't something that happens suddenly on the field when the whistle blows and the crowds roar. Winning is something that builds physically and mentally every day that you train and every night that you dream." —Emmitt Smith

Very few achievements will occur in your life without setting goals and pursuing your dreams. In fact, setting goals should be a natural part of day-to-day living for anyone seeking to achieve personal or business success. For a high school or college athlete, that goal is usually to one day make it big in the professional leagues like the NBA, NFL,

MLB, or NHL. Every actor aspires to be chosen to play a leading role in a major studio film or network television series. The ambitious executive prepares to someday be a vice president or even CEO of his company. While setting goals plays an important role in achieving our dreams, many people are often overly focused on reaching their goals and don't prepare themselves to actually deal with the radically changed circumstances of their lives that will occur once they reach those goals.

How many times have you seen an athlete, actor, or businessperson seemingly on top of the world only to drown in a financial cesspool as a result of not being able to navigate the waters of success? As an observer, I often ask myself two questions: *Why does it appear that so many people cannot hold on to their success? And how early in life did that person's preparation for life after success start?*

I have been blessed over the years with tremendous chances to personally improve and advance my life. I grew up in a single-parent home in middle class, blue-collar neighborhoods in and around Cincinnati, Ohio, with my one younger brother, Mark. My mother Angel and father Douglas divorced when I was only three but, despite that, my family unit was strong. We lived with my mother while my father spent many years in the military, but I always knew I had the love and support of both parents, and my brother and I always felt cared for and loved by our extended family community of several cousins, aunts, and uncles, along with my mother's mother, Grandma Birdie C. Hudson, and my father's mother, Grandma Reva Miller.

One of my earliest memories of childhood was that I never really enjoyed school very much because I hated the idea of standardized tests. It concerned me that they would be used to determine my worth as a student, and I was suspicious of the dubious insight they provided regarding my chances of succeeding in the future. Like a lot young African American kids growing up in middle America, I was absolutely terrified by the whole notion that I could possibly fail and be labeled a "bad student" or "not likely to succeed." From my young point of view, the educational system was hardly kind to students who struggled and had a difficult time grasping the fundamentals. These students were frequently set aside and minimized, unfairly positioned to never realize their fullest potential. They weren't given adequate educational support to change their destiny. The real threat of being labeled as one of those types of kids freaked me out and honestly scared me straight into working like Rocky Balboa, running those endless stairs in the movie *Rocky* in an all-out effort to never, *ever* fail.

It seems that as early as I can remember, I feared failure, but I always managed to do well in school. But still, I always resented the fact that no matter how hard I worked, everything I was in the eyes of the Cincinnati Public School

Board of Education, and some of my teachers and peers, came down to exam results that could reverse my prior good work and immediately label me a "failure." Of course, this extreme idea was untrue, but in my impressionable young mind at that time it was as true as the Gospel. I was mortified at the very thought of repeating a grade, and especially horrified at the thought of being trapped in school forever. My disdain for the constricting structure of school was so intense that I secretly practiced, trained, and studied far more than many of my schoolmates.

Ironically, in spite of my rebellious attitude and negative experiences at school, I chose not to outwardly rebel and reject the learning process. Instead, with my mother's encouragement and the grace of almighty God, I was a highly motivated student and actually excelled in school, frequently earning straight A's and a number of awards. I was even named "most outstanding boy" in third grade. I was the valedictorian of my sixth grade class and graduated high school as number five in the top ten in my class based on academic performance. I went on to graduate college Summa Cum Laude from the University of Cincinnati, College Conservatory of Music, and I received my Juris Doctorate Degree from Georgetown University Law Center. By the time I finished Georgetown, I fielded seven employment offers from law firms across the United States.

Given how much I loathed school, I was truly blessed

to have a mother who stressed the importance of making good grades and being prepared. No one can underestimate the significant impact that supportive and caring parents can have on their child's academic education. It is vital for parents to encourage their children to learn and to respect the learning process—even if, like me, the kids are terrified of the institution of school.

As a child, a great source of comfort for me was that I had become a very religious kid intent on building a solid foundation of extended friends and family within our church community. I had, and still have, tremendous faith in God. My dear grandmother, Birdie C. Hudson, introduced us to religion and was the key force in getting my mother, brother, and me heavily involved in the church. We joined the Truth Missionary Baptist Church where my brother and I were baptized. I really fell in love with that church and its extended community. It was like a family to me. Like many entertainers, it was in the church that I began to develop my singing voice. I loved participating in the choir and even had a few solos. It was very exciting to have a chance to go on trips to perform at other churches. I even began to tithe as a child and gave the church ten percent of my allowance and the money I earned in my summer jobs. It was a great time in my life and the period when I first began developing my faith and really understood the value of having spiritually good people around me.

During my childhood, when it came to fame or famous people, I had a very limited understanding of the concept. Like most, I understood fame solely through the lens of popular culture. It was all about athletes, musicians, television, and movie stars. As a child of the '70's, the embodiment of being famous was anybody featured on Robin Leach's *Lifestyles of the Rich and Famous,* athletes, the bands on *American Bandstand* or *Soul Train*, or the stars of *The Brady Bunch, Good Times*, and *All In the Family.* Influenced by glossy magazines, television shows, movies, and the sports pages, I honestly thought fame was about being rich and living an extravagant life in Beverly Hills, while driving around town in a Rolls-Royce. Surely it was a life of exotic travel, fancy restaurants, expensive clothing, and priceless jewelry. I saw the stars and starlets of the music industry, Broadway, and Hollywood as the pinnacle. They were untouchable, glorified beings.

There were several hot musical acts from Ohio I liked when I was a kid—The Isley Brothers, The Ohio Players, Midnight Star, Lakeside, Dazz Band, Slave, Heatwave, Zapp featuring Roger Troutman, and Bootsy Collins. These bands were masters of Rhythm & Blues and soulful funk music and they all went on to have incredible international careers with millions of fans around the world. Although they were not Ohioans, I endlessly dreamed about being a singer and a drummer for Earth Wind & Fire, who were the epitome of musical genius to me. They were truly my "American idols." They embodied my idea of fame and, like most kids who dreamed about being famous, I wanted it too!

My own pursuit of fame took a positive turn in elementary school. My good friend since the fifth grade is actor Roscoe Carroll, professionally known as "Rocky Carroll," who is best known for his television work on the series *Roc, Chicago Hope, NCIS, and NCIS: LA,* and for earning a Tony nomination for his performance in the Broadway production of August Wilson's *Piano Lesson.* He told me about Cincinnati's School for Creative and Performing Arts ("SCPA"). The school was an experimental magnet arts institution developed by the Cincinnati public school system in 1973, designed to promote the arts, academics, and racial integration in the city. SCPA was in fact the first school in the United States that combined a full range of Arts studies with a complete college-preparatory academic program for elementary through high school students. When I was admitted, the school was located across town in the primarily Jewish neighborhood of Roselawn. Students are required to audition to get into the school and less than twenty percent of those who apply each year are actually accepted. The school colors were black and white, which was something that the school took literally by auditioning and enrolling students who had the most promise of becoming successful in the arts and in entertainment. The school recruiters found candidates from the greater Cincinnati metropolitan area with many different ethnic and economic backgrounds.

SCPA proved to be a huge success and has produced several notable graduates including:

- Sarah Jessica Parker: Actress, Emmy and Golden Globe-winning star of *Sex and the City*, four-time Emmy nominee;
- Rebecca Budig: Actress, *Guiding Light*;
- Carmen Electra: Actress, *Baywatch*;
- Nick Lachey, Drew Lachey, and Justin Jeffre of the multi-platinum album group 98 Degrees;
- Rocky Carroll: Tony Award and Emmy Award nominated actor, *NCIS*;
- George Evans: Jazz vocalist, and multi-award-nominated recording artist;
- Cyrus Vorhis: producer of *Bulletproof Monk*, *Kung Fu Panda*, *Robin Hood*, and the Emmy-nominated miniseries, *Sleeper Cell*.

The school was a dream, and proved to be one of the most enriching and life-changing experiences for me personally. It was very different from the mostly urban neighborhood schools I had previously attended. SCPA was, instead, a utopia—a mosaic of white kids, black kids, Asian kids, rich kids, poor kids, straight kids, and gay kids all pursuing artistic excellence.

Most of my clients today are more than familiar with my mantra—*"80% of success is access."*

I regularly say this line as a means of helping them better understand how to succeed, whether it be in Hollywood or in other professions, but, most importantly, in life. SCPA gave me access to a nurturing environment that allowed me to develop my artistic gifts and interact with people from vastly different socioeconomic, cultural, and racial backgrounds. For the first time in my life, I was exposed to new environments, and learned fresh and different points of view, philosophies, and outlooks on life. My world suddenly opened up, and my life was no longer restricted to the confines of my limited, middle-class, blue-collar urban environment. Even more significantly, the performing arts school gave me an outlet to pursue my love for the fine arts. It often distracted me from my deeply held fear of the institution of school that had driven so much of my efforts up to that point. Through SCPA, I was experiencing a transformation—becoming a new person. In retrospect, it was my first experience with the kind of "access" that had the power to forever change the direction and potential of my life.

My experience at SCPA underscored the importance of experiencing new and different environments while growing up, and then later, as an adult. It's one of the most essential ingredients for personal and professional growth. Director

Spike Lee has often talked about how his parents' insistence on taking him and his siblings to Broadway plays and jazz clubs as children shaped him as a filmmaker. Similar parallels can be drawn with the success of actress and singer Vanessa Williams, the daughter of two music teachers who regularly took her to Manhattan to introduce her to the theater. While the students at SCPA were, in so many ways, unique individuals, we were all unified by our deep appreciation for, and dedication to, being excellent in the arts. All of us had an unyielding desire to be the best at our crafts.

I was admitted to SCPA to major in drums and percussion. However, I was trained in several other areas of the arts as a part of the curriculum. Along with playing the drums, I studied drama, musical theater, fine arts, and voice. I starred in numerous school productions, including what is still probably known as one of the school's most successful efforts. I played the Cowardly Lion when our production of the musical *The Wiz* opened at the school. Later, we went on the road in 1981, as a national tour to perform at the National Theatre in Washington, DC.

In many ways, SCPA was very similar to the high school of performing arts in the 1980 hit movie *Fame,* starring Irene Cara. The film came out in my junior year of high school and was the blockbuster of the summer. It seemed as though every teenager in America had seen the movie and was talking about it.

Fame focuses on an ensemble of kids at the New York City High School for the Performing Arts in Manhattan. The theme explores the powerful combination of talented kids, innocence, the performing arts, and the potential for greatness. To me, the film represented the chance for people to make dramatic changes in their lives through the arts. It was so similar to my experiences at SCPA that it deeply resonated with me and with many of my friends. That movie made me reflect for the first time on the very real possibility of getting out of Cincinnati and changing my life forever. Nobody that I grew up with had ever really done it, so the idea seemed implausible at the time, but *Fame* triggered a lot of dreams and opened my eyes to exciting new possibilities.

The film's characters were just trying to figure it all out—just like me. The kids were pursuing their art while living out the most basic concept of fame—"getting there." They learned that if you work hard and develop your craft, you could go on to do exceptional things in life.

But there was much more to be learned from the film. The students in *Fame* also learned about the darker, more unsavory side of the entertainment world—a world where unscrupulous characters prey on the naïveté and deep hunger for success that so many young dreamers possess. It's the kind of world that cost Vanessa Williams her Miss America crown and, arguably, ended the young lives of people like Selena, Tupac Shakur, Biggie Smalls, and River Phoenix.

Although the Academy award-winning theme song for the film contained the lyrics "Fame! I want to live forever," the reality in the film, as in life, is that fame—more often than not—is ephemeral. There is absolutely no guarantee it will last. In fact, one of the first things you learn once you start working regularly in the entertainment and sports business is that it *will* end.

In so many ways, the song from the *Fame* soundtrack that had the most profound impact on me was, "Out Here On My Own." This song was at the center of one of the most riveting scenes, and the soaring melancholy of Cara's solo transformed the movie. It was later played on several national radio stations. It is a song about finding one's sense of place and purpose in the world. It became my personal anthem, because at that point in my life I was living a duality of existence and the lyrics made me think about a few real life issues I had been happily sweeping under the proverbial carpet.

Due to the irreconcilable differences that I had with my mother's then-boyfriend who my brother and I were forced to move in with, I left home when I was sixteen. At that time, my life began to imitate art and "On My Own" was taking on a literal meaning. At school, my life was outwardly still moving along perfectly. I was an A-student and even something of a celebrity among my friends and teachers because of my performances in the school productions.

But at home, my life was crumbling after I walked out. I initially moved in with my grandmother Birdie. Then, later on, I moved in with my aunt Stella Anderson who agreed to take legal custody of me and allowed me to sleep in her basement until my high school graduation. Living in my aunt's basement was a radical change from being home with my mother and brother, but it was not as grim as it may sound—I wasn't stuck in a gloomy basement like the kid in the 1989 horror classic film *The Cellar*. In the Midwest, basements were, and still often are, large refinished living areas where many kids and young adults hang out or live at their parents' home. My aunt's basement included a bedroom that one of her sons had refinished, so I had a comfortable, but not fancy space to call home.

From the age of sixteen on, the arts became my anchor and my plan for success. I completely immersed myself in music and theater; they became the mooring I needed to survive what would have otherwise been a tumultuous existence. When I look back on that time, I can't help but see how fortunate I was to have the arts to keep me focused. Given my tough family situation, I could easily have gone astray and become just another African American young male statistic as a gang member engaging with drugs or some other type of detrimental behavior that has plagued so many of the people I grew up with.

I truly believe that a great deal of my early motivation was once again due to a deep fear of failure and, after I moved out of my mom's house, the stakes were that much higher. I knew if I failed—if I slowed down—there would be no one to pick me up. That was my reality and I accepted it. I had no real place to call home and no real place of refuge, so I learned the beauty of intestinal fortitude. The Swiss-born philosopher Jean-Jacques Rousseau said, "Endurance and to be able to endure is the first lesson a child should learn because it's the one they will most need to know."

Thank God, I had a survivor's instinct. By the time I graduated from high school, I had mastered how to live a dual existence. At school, I was the smiling teenager, acting as if I didn't have a care in the world. But I also knew that when I graduated, my life would come crashing down. I had no real support system that could help me figure out how to deal with life after high school. Like so many of my other family members, my future was inevitably going to be working in a car factory or on some assembly line for a union salary. That was my other reality.

But while it lasted, SCPA and the arts were my access, and the place where I would begin to plant my seeds for success much later in life. One of my fondest memories of SCPA was our outstanding musical theater program. We were known throughout the city and the arts community as "those amazingly talented kids from that arts school."

In addition to putting on elaborate school productions, we often performed at events outside the school such as Christmas caroling in the homes of wealthy patrons of the arts in Cincinnati area. On several occasions, we even traveled to other towns and states to perform with other show choirs and at arts events. Getting a chance to see other communities and to perform in front of enthusiastic audiences was great training for us. Naturally, in our teenage imaginations, we were superstars.

But, in spite of our local notoriety, I was always aware of the fact that this was not the kind of fame that really counted in the grand scheme of things. There was certainly no monetary gain. Fame in school and the local community was not the big leagues. It wasn't Broadway or Hollywood. Our performances often made me wonder, "What if these experiences are it? What if they are the biggest experiences of fame I'll ever have in my life?"

In school, as I looked ahead at my life and pondered what I might become when I grew up, I never really considered pursuing the life of a professional performer. I doubted there were many opportunities available to me in Ohio. Coming from a working class background, my realistic plan was to get that union job after high school.

For the most part, no one in my family ever left Cincinnati. In fact, about ninety-eight percent of my family members still live in the Cincinnati metropolitan area. When I was growing up, even those in my family who were considered college material received their degrees, but *still* went on to work on the assembly lines at Ford, Mead Data Central, Proctor & Gamble, or some other large manufacturer with a reputation for treating their employees reasonably well for a lifetime of work. My uncle Glenn Miller, who was an executive at Proctor & Gamble, was one of the rare exceptions of a family member who didn't work at a physical labor job. In my immediate family, you were expected to finish school, get a good job with good benefits, get married, have kids, and live in the community. That was how our American dream was supposed to unfold. There was no pressure to go to college because an average person at that time could get a good paying labor job and take care of his family.

During that period in America, millions of hardworking people were able to live the American dream, buy a home, and send their kids to college doing factory work. While getting a management office job was possible, those jobs were rarely filled from my neighborhood work pool. God created an incredible universe of jobs and professions for his children, but unfortunately, given the limited experiences and lack of access, most of my family members who I grew up with were not generally focused on going to college. Therefore, like everyone in my family, I was simply planning to work on the assembly line at Ford

Motor Company or at one of the other local factories that were hiring after high school.

At that point in my life, I had not heard of Andy Warhol or his statement about everyone getting fifteen minutes of fame. It was the guidance counselor at SCPA, Mrs. Gwen Fields, who pulled me aside one day. She took me to her office, opened my eyes and put me on the path of discovering my first fifteen minutes of fame. She sat me down and asked, "Darrell, have you ever thought about going to college?"

"No, I haven't," I admitted candidly.

The reality was that, not only was college not necessary in my narrow world, but I couldn't afford it. I didn't know anything about scholarships, financial aid, or grants. I only knew that college was prohibitively expensive for someone like me. Mrs. Fields told me all about financial assistance programs and helped me figure out that, based on my good grades, I could be eligible for scholarships and grants to cover my tuition, books, and housing. With her full encouragement, I applied to some colleges. That experience led me to immediately appreciate the benefits of my hard work. All of my diligence and determination in school was finally paying off. Originally, I just wanted to finish school and get on with my life. It was never even a glimmer in my wildest dreams that I would actually go to college or attend any post-graduate studies. Yet, thanks to Mrs. Fields—and the Lord, of course—a new door had opened in my life. I was about to take a red carpet ride to a new chapter in my life that was incomparable to anything that anyone in my family had ever known or ever could have imagined.

My goal was to pursue a career in voice and musical theater, so I applied to a few different schools in Ohio and out of state before I ultimately decided to go to the University of Cincinnati, College Conservatory of Music ("CCM"). It had an excellent reputation as one of the best and most selective music conservatories in the country. The voice and musical theater programs were widely considered among the top in the nation, and it was right there in my hometown. When I received my acceptance letter to CCM, along with a full scholarship with on-campus housing, it was my first real "dream come true moment." CCM is known for producing many noted vocal and musical theatre stars like the opera diva Kathleen Battle, actor Dorian Harwood, and Shoshana Bean, known for her role of Elphanba in *Wicked*.

As I was getting ready to start CCM and move out of my aunt Stella's basement, I remember thinking, "Wow, if that one meeting with one person like Mrs. Fields could change my life, what other opportunities will become available to me if I continue to work hard and continue to meet new people?" When I really thought about it, there were others from SCPA who played key roles in opening my eyes to new possibilities and opportunities in life. People like Susie Louiso (formally Susie Schwartz), the PR person in the

Artistic Director's Office who was like a second mother to me, and her three daughters—Janie, Lynnie, and Nancy—were like my sisters. Susie was one of the smartest and most connected people I had ever met. She and her family always looked out for me and were supportive beyond anything I could have imagined.

I went to college believing that there just might be a path to success through the arts. I didn't know what form it would take, but I could at least sense the possibilities. I believed in my heart that there just might be other people like Gwen Fields and Susie Schwartz, who could guide me to that path, so I resolved to continue to work hard, stay focused, and keep the faith. I was still motivated by the fear of failure, so early on I started thinking about how I could maintain my success if I ever actually achieved it.

I was at CCM with students who were considered the best and the brightest from all across America. We had all come together to pursue a common dream: to become a professional artist. We were learning what it would take to make it. CCM was the next step to pursuing what we all thought at the time was "fame." Later, buoyed by my experiences at SCPA, as well as the support of the extended family from SCPA, I honestly believed that I had the potential to hit it big. And if God was willing to bless me with that opportunity, I was very determined not to ever let it be taken away.

During my sophomore year at CCM, everyone at school was auditioning and interviewing for different musical theater opportunities apart from the conservatory, at regional theater companies around the United States, cruise ships, and theme parks. I also sought to secure summer employment and landed a job in my sophomore year as a resident ensemble member with the Civic Light Opera in Pittsburgh, Pennsylvania ("CLO"). I actually had the privilege of working at the CLO for three summers where I performed in over twenty-one musical theatre productions. My senior year, I even got a chance to go on the road with a summer stock tour of *Guys and Dolls*, starring Maureen McGovern and Tony Roberts. Through performing in the shows at the CLO, I was able to gain professional experience, while simultaneously building my confidence as a performer. I also made what felt to me at the time like a ton of money. I was a bona fide professional actor and member of the Actor's Equity Association and making a real salary which, in turn, enabled me to support myself and start a savings account.

In reflection, I would say that getting into CCM and performing with the CLO was my first fifteen minutes of fame but, at the time, I was just enjoying the experience and praying that it would last. Realistically, I did not believe that everyone automatically got fifteen minutes of fame. At SCPA, in the movie *Fame*, and at CCM, I was educated about the harsh reality that many performers live through. I saw that there were far more artists who were losers than winners in the fame game, and I was keenly aware that only a few people would get a chance at real success. However, as an eternal optimist, I was determined to be one of them. Yet, I was not naïve. I was always aware of the fact that the odds were against me. So, with that understanding, I pursued my dream with commitment and passion, and I never looked back. In my mind, I believed I had no other choice but to succeed and that my real challenge was to figure out how to sustain my success. Relying on my gift of endurance, I also knew that on my quest, if I did not reach my goal, I could at least say with conviction that I had given it my all. Furthermore, I had already reaped the benefits of genuine hard work and study. I was fortunate to have an excellent education I could rely on.

Since then, I have learned that nothing beats preparation and that education can open up many doors to your life. There are far too many young people pursuing careers in entertainment and sports who don't realize the role that a good education can play in creating opportunities and providing a solid foundation for a long-term career. During my years of practicing law and working in the industry as an artist, I have learned that people who successfully sustain their success often train themselves to be prepared, both mentally and creatively. These people understand that developing a strategy for maintaining success is a key component to still being around after their fifteen minutes of fame have come to an end. Possessing even the greatest talent is rarely enough to sustain success. You must condition your mind early on your path to success, and you must also have a solid business strategy to be around for the sixteenth minute of fame.

Perhaps William Shakespeare said it best when he wrote: "All things are ready, if our minds be so."

Chapter 3

REVEALING YOUR FIFTEEN MINUTES OF FAME

Circumstance does not make the man; it reveals him to himself. —James Allen, *As a Man Thinketh*

We've discussed the concept of the fifteenth minutes of fame a great deal, but what we haven't discussed is how to recognize it. It might seem surprising, but often when success is finally achieved, people have no idea that their time has arrived and the fruits of success are ripe for the picking. And even of those who do have some understanding of the place they've come to, in many cases don't know how to leverage their success before their fifteen minutes are up. Over the years it has become clear to me that achieving fame should not be the real focus. It's far more critical to understand that for every effort it takes to become famous or successful, it takes ten times more effort to stay famous or to stay successful. And the key starting point of all of this is recognizing when you're sitting in your prime. Then you can begin the real work of getting ready for life after the high point of that success or fame is gone.

Before we get ahead of ourselves, I'm not about to promise you the quick and easy way to anticipate when your fifteen minutes will happen. There is no exact formula that can anticipate when your big break will come. It's not as if you will get some secret message from God telling you that it will be next Friday or on your birthday. And even though there will be no lightning bolts or rolls of thunder, you must be open to the possibility that it could happen to you at any time. *You must be ready to take full advantage of it in the most productive way.*

As you work toward your goal, there are times when you may feel like you are just going through the motions to get to the end of a project, a job, or an experience. You really don't expect whatever you're involved in to be the big break that will change your life in any meaningful way. Yet there are other times when you absolutely know that you are at a critical moment in your life. You have reached the crossroads you have been working hard for and, if you make the right choices, it could lead to the kind of positive change that you have been waiting a long time to achieve.

On the other hand, if you make the wrong choices, it could affect your future adversely and you're back to the struggle of pursuing your goal.

Being at that serious stage in your career can manifest itself in many ways depending on who you are and what your profession is. For a young comedy actor looking to take his career to the next level, it could mean deciding to take a serious dramatic role for the next project—whether that's with a major studio or with a low-budget independent film. If the actor believes that the drama project has the real potential to win him much-desired critical acclaim, it may be his golden opportunity to finally break out of the pack and shine even if it wasn't the way he anticipated the "big break" happening.

I am a big proponent of separating yourself from the pack and taking chances in order to achieve your goals. If possible, you must distinguish yourself or find a way to make sure you're not just settling with the status quo out of either fear of change or fear of failure. An honest self-evaluation will allow you to determine if you're just gliding along in life. It can also be the first step toward "revealing your fifteen minutes of fame." In fact, the self-examination aspect of the process will be the most important step you take in learning how to sustain your goals. Understanding who you are and what you need to change most in your life will allow you to break away from the trap of achieving your goals without broadening your vision.

Socrates once wrote, "The unexamined life is not worth living." And while this great thinker's philosophy on life might seem harsh and absolute, the fact that it still resonates over two thousand years later is a testament to its element of truth. If you want to achieve any level of success, you must probe your mind, look deep within, and ask yourself the tough questions:

- How will I ever become the greatest I can be?
- How will I know whether I am at a place that has the potential to propel my career or my life to the next level?
- How will I know what I should do when I actually get to the next level so that I can continue or sustain my growth?

Following my graduation from CCM, I moved to New York City and embarked on my personal journey to discover my early opportunities for fame. I was Broadway-bound— well, at least Bronx-bound for the moment. I certainly couldn't afford Manhattan's exorbitant rents and artist-unfriendly cost of living, so I moved to a small, low-rent apartment in an Old World Jewish neighborhood with my high school friend and valedictorian Ethan Tucker. The Bronx is a borough north of Manhattan known in hip-hop slang as the Boogie Down Bronx, which is the birthplace of hip-hop and Grandmaster Flash.

New York was a total culture shock, as all the classic stereotypes of New York life seemed to invade my mind on a daily basis. I eventually adjusted, but for some time I was sure that everyone around me was a thief, a murderer, or some psychopath who was going to mug me—or worse.

Like most struggling performers in New York, I set out to look for a "regular" job to sustain myself. I needed cash—after all, I had to eat and keep a roof over my head until I found acting work. But I held true to one hard and fast rule: Never, ever wait tables for survival—not that there's anything innately wrong with being a waiter. It's honest work. Many great people have waited tables for a living and still do so today. It was simply that I was uncomfortable with the whole idea of serving people as a waiter. It felt much too much like a negative stereotype—African Americans before me had served masters without any real freedom of choice to do otherwise. Admittedly, it was a type of service position that just weighed on me.

At one time, I was determined to put aside my antipathy and actually did try waiting tables once. It was a total fiasco. In fact, I had one of the worst experiences a waiter could ever have when I accidently dropped a strawberry daiquiri all over the son of the famous jazz pianist Bob James. It was an absolute nightmare and exactly the type of service experience I had dreaded.

Motivated by my philosophy on work and the need to find gainful employment, I managed to get a job as a personal trainer at a health club during the day and put my blue-collar roots to work at night unloading packages for a New Jersey Trucking company that was run by a fellow actor's dad. Although my work schedule was grueling, I remained full of optimism and excitement about a career in musical theater. I truly believed I had as much promise as the next guy. Besides, things had worked out pretty well for me up to that point. I felt like my life had taken some inexplicable, unpredictable magic carpet ride. I was anxious to see where that magic carpet would take me next, even though I was still fearful that the adventurous ride would come to a screeching halt.

After touring with a couple of national production companies and performing the lead role in an original jazz opera entitled, "Leo," I landed one of the principle roles in an international tour of the musical *The Princess and the Pea* set to travel to India, Sri Lanka, and other countries where the United States sought to promote cultural exchanges through the arts. Now, it's important to know that this was the mid-1980s when the United States was at war with Libya, and a terror alert had been issued for travel within the region. Several people turned down the tour— understandably—fearful of the potential danger. I was not among them. I was far too excited about performing on stage in an international touring production and the chance to travel outside the United States to pass on this opportunity.

In show business you must be willing to pay your dues, and I knew that this role would be important to my long-term strategy of making it in musical theater. I was willing to take a risk, and I refused to let short-term thinking or fear stop me from taking full advantage of a potentially life-changing experience. I confidently believed life could not have been better. My fifteen minutes were arriving and nothing and no one—not even terrorists—were going to stop them!

Thank God I made that decision. The tour proved to be more awe-inspiring than I could have ever dreamed. We were treated like celebrities by the various host embassies responsible for arranging the tour, and the audiences gave us standing ovations. I felt like royalty during the performances, but I was blown away and horrified by the abject poverty I observed in some of the countries we visited. It really made me appreciate even the few possessions I had back in the States. It's incredible how seeing the world from a new perspective can help you value your life that much more and realize how fortunate you have been all along. I'll never forget how blessed I felt standing in front of some of the greatest wonders of the world, from the ancient pyramids along the Nile in Egypt to the majestic Taj Mahal in India. What an incredible opportunity to experience life the world over. Life could indeed be phenomenal. After all, I was just a guy from Ohio—Darrell Miller from across the river in Cincinnati—whose father moved out when he was three years old and who slept in his aunt's basement. Without the encouragement of my high school guidance counselor, I would, without a doubt, have been working on an assembly line instead of traveling with a musical performance company half a world away.

It was in India where I had my epiphany in Bombay (now called Mumbai) at about 5:30 in the morning. I had wandered out to watch the locals do their morning chores. As I stood on the shore of the Arabian Sea reflecting on how far I had come since leaving my home in Ohio, I realized I was experiencing a breakthrough. *I began to accept the fact that life could present an infinite number of good possibilities for me.* Those opportunities could essentially be boundless and were within my reach, waiting for me to make the most of them.

Up to that point, I had just been going with the flow, expecting that one day I would suddenly wake up from this wonderful dream and find myself back in my aunt's basement in Cincinnati. But now I had an awareness of the potentials and possibilities around me. I wondered: *What if the ride doesn't have to end? What if I have a steering wheel and can control my own destiny?*

I began to believe the Lord had something more in store for me than just being a performer— that perhaps there was a way for me to invest all of the achievements and opportunities I had thus far experienced into even more successful endeavors.

"But just how can I do that?"

Chapter 4

MY SIXTEENTH MINUTE

"Harry, get them to sing your song, and they will want to know who you are.

And if they want to know who you are, you've gained the first step in bringing truth and bringing insight that might help people get through this rather difficult world." —Paul Robeson to Harry Belafonte[11]

In college, I recall the day clearly that Worth Gardner, my professor who chaired the musical theater program, asked our directing class if anyone had heard of Paul Robeson. You could hear a pin drop in the room. The forty upperclassmen—including only two African-Americans—had no answer.

The professor asked again, "You mean *no one* knows who Paul Robeson is?"

Once more, not a single person raised their hand or ventured an answer. Incensed at our ignorance, Professor Gardner promptly accused us of being dumb kids who did not think beyond our own little song and dance numbers. He then proceeded to assign the class a thirty-page paper on Robeson over the weekend—to be delivered the following Monday. I will never forget how terrified we all felt—so much so that my buddy and I felt driven to pull an all-nighter to complete our papers.

The experience proved to be an awakening for me. I was forced to open my eyes and learn about one of the greatest Americans in our history. Robeson was an all-American football player, a twelve-time letterman at Rutgers, and a Columbia University-trained lawyer. Robeson would go on to become a widely acclaimed actor discovered by the great playwright Eugene O'Neil, who, with his fateful decision to cast him in his play *The Emperor Jones*, made Robeson the first African-American to star on Broadway. Robeson later became an international recording artist and film star, enthralling audiences around the world with his deep bass voice as he sang in numerous languages. Reaching far beyond the stage, screen, and record albums, Robeson would ultimately become one of the world's greatest civil rights activists, selflessly using his fame and influence to speak on behalf of the world's oppressed and downtrodden. Given his gifts, Robeson could have been a professional football player, a high stakes financier, or a practicing attorney. He was a true Renaissance man.

Professor Gardner's disappointment and irritation with his students was certainly warranted. I was also shocked to learn that this man who had accomplished so much came perilously close to having it all taken away from him in the 1950s during the McCarthy era. It was a dark period in our nation's history when the U.S. government, led by the questionable efforts of Senator Eugene McCarthy, carried out a crackdown on Americans—artists and entertainers were especially singled out—and accused them of having Communist leanings. A large number of those accused were cruelly blacklisted for many long years.

Although he never conceded any ties to that affiliation, Robeson himself was charged with being a Communist. He was summarily stripped of his good name and his passport, and was further denied almost all of his accomplishments, all of which resulted in an almost complete erasure of his extraordinary legacy from the American history books. That terrible injustice profoundly horrified Professor Gardner and compelled him to educate his students on the remarkable life of this great man.

Studying Paul Robeson's path to fame motivated me to stretch my own personal limits. Here was an African-

American man who was born in the late nineteenth century to a runaway slave—a man who would go on to achieve lofty heights and would be awarded with the kind of fame and fortune few people on the planet ever achieve. Robeson tasted true greatness, only to see it all wiped out by the ignorant and narrow beliefs of powerful people who abused their influence over the nation. At the pinnacle of his success in the 1940s, he was arguably as famous as Michael Jackson and Bill Cosby were in the 1980s and as Jay Z, Denzel Washington, Will Smith, or Oprah Winfrey are today—all rolled into one. But living at a time when racial discrimination was rampant and so pervasive throughout society, Robeson had many more obstacles to overcome than those well-known African Americans of later more enlightened decades.

Robeson was not distracted by the privileges his talents afforded him. He was keenly aware that his fame as a singer and actor could best be utilized in advancing the cause of civil rights in this country and the world. His deeply ingrained moral compass told him that there was a greater call to the service of his people than just his own personal achievement. A man of utmost conviction, Robeson chose to jeopardize the comforts of his career in order to continue to protest against the injustices he saw in America, including the crime of lynching and racial discrimination. Putting his worldly achievements to positive use, Robeson stood steadfast on principle.

Repeatedly asked if he was a Communist by suspicious and questionably moral politicians during the infamous McCarthy hearings held by the House Committee on Un-American Activities, Robeson firmly refused to answer the direct question, but he responded: "This is the basis, and I am not being tried for whether I am a Communist, I am being tried for fighting for the rights of my people, who are still second-class citizens in this United States of America.[12]

Robeson could have easily saved his own reputation and perhaps even been left alone by his detractors had he chosen to speak out against communism. Instead, he chose to use his fame to help break down the laws that prohibited almost all other people of color from being treated as equal citizens. At the time, it was a pipe-dream for an African-American kid to even think about becoming president of the United States, the CEO of a Fortune 500 company, the head coach of an NFL football team, or a Broadway star—let alone attending a decent school across town with kids who didn't necessarily look like him. None of those opportunities happened by chance. They required the efforts and sacrifice of people like Robeson and, later, Martin Luther King Jr., Malcolm X, and countless others who gave their lives in the fight for justice and equality among all Americans. Robeson paid an enormous price for his sacrifice and resolute stance on civil rights. Tragically, he suffered from severe depression and never fully reclaimed his career. He would have continued to remain unknown but for Professor Gardener who taught me, and all of my other classmates, that Paul Robeson was a man of extraordinary depth and integrity who should never be forgotten.

As I inhaled the bracing, salty air of the Arabian Sea on that pivotal morning in India, it was my knowledge and sincere appreciation of Robeson's extraordinary accomplishments that I remembered so clearly. Aware that my prior achievements had been haphazard and unpredictable, I knew at that moment I wanted to assure myself of future success. Little did I know that I was at the infancy stage in the process of discovering how to get to the sixteenth minute of fame. Looking back, I recall that while I was enjoying life in my shining hour, I instinctively knew that I wanted to discover ways to continue to travel around the world and have experiences as profound as those I was blessed to be having. And as a young black man in America, I wanted to take full advantage of the opportunities that were unfolding before me and were within my reach during my fifteen minutes. I wanted my magic carpet to go as far as it could possibly go and then fly on a little further.

For the first time, I began to consider that, perhaps like Robeson, there was more to my life than being a performer. I reasoned that perhaps continuing to take my chances as an actor in New York City was not the best way to achieve my goal. The erratic and unreliable process of achieving success on the stage left far too much to chance. There was just too much dumb and blind luck involved, and I wanted more control over my destiny. I wanted to continue my life's journey without being vulnerable to the capricious demands of casting agents, producers, and directors, and the unpredictable whims of the mercurial entertainment industry in general. With much consideration, I decided that I would pursue new career possibilities beyond theater.

It was back at that transformative moment on the Indian shore that I began to explore all the exciting possibilities for my life. I began to search for options that could set me on a new and phenomenal course and take my present success to the next level. Like my hero Paul Robeson, I knew I had the ability to do a lot more with the fifteen minutes of fame that I had worked so hard for.

When I returned from the tour, I began researching alternative professions, although due to my continuing love affair with theater, I first thought about becoming a theater producer so I could arrange international tours of hit shows. However, in order to be able to finance all types of theatrical projects, including musicals, dramas, comedies, and revivals, I wanted to find a way to become independently wealthy so I could do it all. Earnestly considering the best way to achieve my goal, I came up with the most historically reliable path that every parent in America at that time wished for each of their children—I would become a doctor or lawyer.

In spite of my prior resentment and disdain for school, once I had some distance from the classroom with its tiresome term papers, standardized tests, and grueling exams, I really began to appreciate the intrinsic value of education and additional schooling. I saw how my education had shaped me intellectually, had strengthened my mind and, ultimately, how it had broadened my perspective on life. In truth, it was mainly because of my education that I was able to find myself on the other side of the world performing an American live-stage musical with a talented cast on an international tour.

I began to evaluate professional schools, starting my career research with medical school. I quickly concluded that it would take me out of the entertainment field far too long for my liking, so I decided to explore the possibility of becoming a lawyer instead. A big plus about obtaining a law degree was that law school would only take three years versus the four years of medical school followed by additional years of interning and residency before I could actually start my own practice (or, more accurately, make real money) as a doctor. I extended my research and examined the role that lawyers play in entertainment, learning that they were an essential part of the very fabric of the industry. Not only were attorneys involved in making the deals and structuring the all-important contracts, but many of the lawyers of the past had gone on to become the studio heads. "Super lawyers" like Thomas Phillip Pollock, who was chairman at MCA Universal at one time, and Frank Wells, who was the then president of the Walt Disney Company, often became the chief decision makers and producers of their day. Their keen understanding of the pragmatic economics of the business and their considerable financial resources had strategically positioned them to rise to the top.

This new discovery was like a light bulb going on in my head. I was convinced that once I finished law school I would be able to apply my legal skills to the entertainment industry. It was ideal—as a lawyer I could sustain my fifteen minutes and then get to my sixteenth minute and beyond.

I applied to twelve law schools, ranging from the highly improbable and rather lofty Harvard, to the far more probable excellent state schools like the University of Minnesota, Ohio State University and University of Michigan. Thankfully, I was accepted to nine of the twelve schools, and even granted a full scholarship with the University of Minnesota. I was all set to head to Minnesota when I received an application in the mail from the Dean of Admissions at Georgetown University Law Center who considered me to be a very promising candidate and invited me to apply. I was truly honored. After all, Georgetown University Law Center is one of the most prestigious schools in the country. But at the time, I had already spent over a thousand dollars on law school applications and I could not afford to pay one more application fee. Luckily, the law center had a policy of waiving your fee if you could provide them with a good reason. I certainly had more than a mere "good" reason, and thinking outside the box for an honest explanation and a unique appeal for dispensation, I chose to write: *I am surviving in New York City.* That was my exact answer to the question. For a Cincinnati kid migrating to the Big Apple, this answer was no joke, but an unqualified truth.

Remarkably, it worked. The school waived my fee, I applied, and I was accepted to Georgetown for enrollment in the fall of 1987.

I chose Georgetown not only because of the excellent reputation of the school but also because I believed that graduating from a nationally recognized law school would open more doors for me after graduation. Also, being in our nation's capitol afforded me an amazingly rare opportunity to study American laws within walking distance of each of our branches of government. After all, Washington is an international city and the epicenter of the American legal system. On a more personal level, my father lived minutes away from DC in southern Maryland, and it would be a tremendous opportunity to try to reconnect with him.

Law school was, by far, one of the hardest endeavors I had ever attempted in my life. The course load was intense and everyone was constantly living in their own private hell.

The school used the demanding Socratic Method of teaching law students that was right out of the old classic film *The Paper Chase*. Many times I wanted to give up, as I struggled with my natural antipathy toward organized education and chafed against its structures and confinements. But somehow I kept going forward.

While attending law school, I lived with my father during my first year, which is something I had not done since spending the whole summer of 1979 with him when I was fifteen. That long ago summer had been a really fun time, especially after my dad bought me my first car. But now that I was an adult, living with him did present its tough moments and sometimes we clashed. However, I also learned that we had some similarities. One main point of commonality was our sense of discipline. My father retired from the military as a Sergeant Major of the U.S. Army, which is the highest enlisted rank, so discipline was a major part of his life. The open racism, unjust laws, and limited opportunities for African-Americans in this country had forced him to the back of the bus when he was growing up in Cincinnati, but he made no excuses. My father persevered and never allowed himself to become a failure in a system that was unfairly designed for him to fail. Interestingly, although he was not around much when I was growing up, somehow this essential aspect of his nature was passed on to me. It was my father's strong character, work ethic, and the abiding faith that it would all be worth it in the long run which helped me get through my darkest days of law school.

After graduating from Georgetown and securing my first full-time job as an attorney, I began to more fully comprehend the biggest life lesson I had learned: *An integral part of the sixteenth minute of fame is being ready to accept change and opportunity.*

I never grew up dreaming of being a lawyer. My eyes were directly focused on the stage. But by opening my field of vision and thinking outside the proverbial box, more and more opportunities unfolded for me.

All too often many people in our society are so intensely focused on one particular avenue to a specific goal that they completely miss out on other paths that appear, or other great opportunities that may arise along the way.

It all begins with keeping an open mind.

Oftentimes, we think about our goals so linearly that we miss the signs signaling slight detours that could lead to bigger and better things. For instance, the playwright coveting a Tony award on Broadway passes on an opportunity to adapt her play into a screenplay for a film director ready to sign her to the project. The film director is so narrowly fixated on directing a feature film that he turns down opportunities to direct commercials, stubbornly ignoring the fact that they could very well establish his sixteenth minute and lead him on to not only direct films but to start his own ad agency as well.

Your ultimate goal is to be around for the sixteenth minute.

In retrospect, it seems as though every time I took a chance on faith to try something different or to keep myself open to new possibilities, great things happened that I had never envisioned. For me, it reinforced the old notion of the importance of preparation for the inevitable *fifteen minutes of fame* that was certain to occur.

"Will I get my fifteen minutes?" you ask.

I believe the answer is "Yes."

But will you make it to the sixteenth minute?

That's the bigger question.

Chapter 5

MAXIMIZING YOUR FIFTEEN MINUTES OF FAME

*After I won the Oscar, my salary doubled,
my friends tripled, my children became more
popular at school, my butcher made a pass at
me, and my maid hit me up for a raise.*
—Shirley Jones

It's essential that you first thoroughly exploit your fifteen minutes of fame before they are over or you may not have a minute beyond that. In fact, missteps that people make when they go from "rags-to-riches–to-rags" might have been avoided had they been more focused and prepared to take full advantage of their opportunities while in the spotlight.

Many of the fallen have suffered at the hands of bad associations and bad advice. When it comes to getting the most out of your fifteen minutes and making the best of your opportunities, it's often your family, friends, and business associates who will determine how well you perform in those fifteen minutes and whether or not you will be able to transition successfully to the sixteenth minute and beyond. There's an old adage that we are judged by the company we keep: Show me your friends and associates and I will show you who you truly are. The same philosophy could be applied to our business relationships. The team of advisors you assemble says a lot about who you are, where you want to be, and where you're going.

Most successful artists, athletes, executives, and leaders of business and politics surround themselves with very competent and trusted advisors from the very start of their success.

When you examine the downfall of many achievers, it's not uncommon for their paths to be littered with ill-advised personal choices and crowded with the wrong friends and associates. In many cases, these associations date back to childhood or young adult life. One can attribute this practice to basic human behavior—it's only natural that most of us want to grow up, become successful, and have our friends and family from the old neighborhood recognize our accomplishments and cheer us on.

But success can be quite daunting for a lot of people. This is particularly true with first generation success when there's a lot of new money, new faces, and new opportunities coming all at once. Flush with fame and fortune, many choose to surround themselves with familiar people as a form of comfort. Athletes and artists, in particular, often choose to anchor themselves with the people they knew long before they hit it big if for no other reason than to maintain some sense of identity and concept of grounded reality.

It's hard to argue that maintaining some sense of self through family members and old friends does not have its merits, but there can be pluses and minuses to these kinds of relationships. Choosing such close alliances without exercising sound reason and judgment can backfire in a most painful way. Bringing bad people or dead weight along for the ride as you advance in your career can create enormous problems for you in the long run. Remember the financial ruin of hip-hop artist M.C. Hammer who reportedly had a lavish entourage in excess of 200 people? There is nothing wrong with having a reasonably sized posse of family and friends along for the ride. But it can be very productive to ask yourself if those family members and friends riding solely on your success may ultimately drain your resources and cost your brand too much to bankroll.

"A man of many companions may come to ruin, but there is a friend who sticks closer than a brother" (Proverbs 18:24).[13]

Whether or not you're a Christian, this principle is quite universal—not everyone deserves to be in your inner circle or even on your team. The Michael Vick story is a perfect example of someone who reportedly allowed old associations and old behaviors to severely damage, if not ruin his career. There's a quote I like about success and money that has stuck with me for a very long time. I cannot recall who said it first, but to paraphrase: *"Success and money do not really change you. They just highlight who you truly are. If you are basically a good person without money, then you become a good person with money and fame. However, if you are a bad person without money, then you become even worse with money and fame."*

Essentially, there are people with good common sense and moral fiber who just so happen to be poor. When those people find success and money, they still have that good common sense and moral fiber, albeit with greater financial resources. They remain people you admire and want to call a friend. On the other hand, there are those people who often demonstrate poor judgment and questionable integrity. When those people reach some level of noteworthy accomplishment and financial gain, their poor behavioral habits do not suddenly disappear; instead, they are often illuminated. The "bad boy" rock star that trashes his hotel room is usually indulged by everyone around him. His destructive antics are magnified and made public because you now have someone with money enjoying some level of notoriety that also has some pretty bad habits. Put simply, if you're a jerk without money, you're probably going to be an even bigger jerk when you have it. Most likely, you were a jerk all along. It's just that now the whole world knows it. Here are three fundamental truisms I've learned about money:

1. Money may not change certain aspects of our core values or our core essence but in fact, money does change things; it changes one's circumstances.

2. Money provides us with greater resources and opportunities. It opens doors never before opened. It can afford us a lifestyle and comforts never before possessed. It gives us an opportunity to help people and causes we may not have been able to support in the past.

3. Money also changes those people around you. Some people will only want to associate with you because you have money and they want the benefits that go along with that.

Basically, you must be aware of your old bad habits and unproductive friends during your fifteen minutes of fame to avoid falling into a trap that will inevitably limit your potential to fully maximize your fifteen minutes. In addition, think about whether or not money underscores the values you have that are positive, or only serves to strengthen the more negative aspects of your personality.

In my years as an attorney, I have seen several people who have come into my office excited about the prospect of me representing them, and they're eager to tell me of their dreams and goals. They talk about all of the wonderful things they're going to do and how they're going to change the world. We have all been around these people before, and although I have heard these same stories on endless occasions, I always listen attentively. My initial response is one of positive encouragement, "Yes, that's possible, and I believe it can happen if *you* believe and work hard to make it happen." But, I also go on to explain to them that my experience tells me if I put $10 million in the middle of the table, more often than not their lofty beliefs, desires, goals, and aspirations would radically change.

So the question becomes, *"How will your goals and beliefs change when the money's on the table?"*

When it comes to choosing your inner circle of friends and business associates, many of those important choices are driven by your core values. It is imperative that you consider people who are your real supporters and those who have shown some level of genuine support for you, your dreams, and your endeavors over a sustained period of time. You can always find people who will walk the red carpet with you, or who will only be there to grab the front row seats at the stadium for your ballgames or opening nights—courtesy of you, of course. But we all need honest, dependable, and *loyal* people in our lives who will be with us through life's inevitable ups and downs. We need those friends who will be by our side when the storms of life unleash their fury around us. We especially need them when the red carpet is gone and the front row tickets are no more. In other words, if you are determined to be the best you can be and to stick around for your sixteenth minute, you need people in your life who will stick by you no matter what. Let's face it, life happens, and much of life can be challenging and unpleasant, so we need committed friends who will ride out the bumps of life with us—certainly not those who only want to be around for the party and the bright lights.

In evaluating your relationships, it's also important to consider advisors who have experiences that are compatible and relevant to you at your new level of achievement. Frequently, these people are mentors, parents, aunts and uncles, coaches, teachers, clergymen, or anyone who has taken a particular interest in your personal growth and development over the years. They can be tremendous resources for you as you seek to navigate new and unfamiliar territory. As you move forward, it's important that you always remain anchored and maintain an ongoing dialogue with those in your professional life who will love and support you whether you're a movie star, MVP of the Super Bowl, or a cashier at the supermarket. Like your inner circle of friends, these special people are always in your corner. They are fiercely loyal and have your back and long-term success as their goal.

In the case of Michael Vick, I often wonder if his circle of friends, associates, and mentors included anyone who valued him enough as a person or who had enough influence over him to guide him away from such potentially career-ending activities as illegal dog fighting. Where were the trusted advisors, good friends, or family members "who knew him when"—if any existed, and who cared enough about his long-term success to help him avoid engaging in old habits? When it was all said and done, Vick had the most to lose, and has clearly suffered the most personally, professionally, and financially from his choices. He lost the adulation of his fans, his $130 million ten-year contract, as well as several lucrative endorsement agreements.

Additionally, one only has to imagine the emotional toll prison takes on a man's spirit and self-worth. Based on news reports, it appears that Vick's associates abandoned him almost overnight. There's no indication of any loyalty to him at all. No doubt some of his so-called friends were saying, "I told you so." Some might have a sympathetic view of Vick as a person who senselessly squandered away his talents and opportunities. However you view it, Michael Vick's story is a sobering lesson for us all.

Our business circles are just as important as our personal relationships. I participated in a panel discussion on the business of entertainment some time ago and I posed this question: *How do people start making bad decisions?*

In my opinion, many people start making bad decisions by hiring bad representation, or more accurately, hiring advisors, agents, and/or other representations who are more invested in the deal on the table than they are in the person they represent. When you hire someone as your attorney, agent, manager, accountant, or publicist who is a poorly qualified person and who is not concerned about your personal growth, it can become a case of the blind leading the blind. You are "blind" to the true motives that drive your representatives, and these representatives are "blind" to your personal goals, challenges, dreams, habits (good or bad), and long-term plans.

Before leaping into any form of representation, it is fundamentally important to understand the role each person plays in your career, the terms under which you should enter those relationships, and whether or not the rep is invested in you personally or the deal that you are about to make.

The Talent/Player Agent

Talent/Player agents are extremely important for those seeking careers as actors, directors, producers, screenwriters, playwrights, authors, or professional athletes. They also represent news anchors, voiceover artists, commercial visual artists, photographers, deejays, and a number of other professions. The talent/player agent's primary job description is rather clear and simple: *Find the client work or get the client in the room with potential buyers*. In essence, this agent's role is to secure employment for their client.

For their services, talent agents in the entertainment industry are paid a fee of ten percent of gross earnings for actors, directors, producers, and writers. Book agents typically receive fifteen percent of an author's gross earnings. Sports agents generally receive up to four percent of gross compensation paid to an athlete under a playing services contract and another fifteen to thirty percent of gross compensation of an athlete's endorsement and marketing contracts.

Since a talent/player agent is partly responsible for helping you put food on the table, you can see why it's rather vital to take your time and approach selecting an agent with the utmost care and due diligence. Make sure you find an agent who not only has a track record, but is willing to use that track record for your benefit and *not* just the benefit of the agent's top-paying clients. I often tell clients that if you sign with an agent solely because of who they represent without getting an action plan from them to represent you in your own personal career, then you are probably going to want to fire that agent within a year.

The Personal Manager

In the entertainment industry, while the agent finds the work, it is the manager's task to advise the client on the creative aspects of their career and, in some cases, to manage the personal affairs of the client. In other words, the manager ultimately provides career advice and guidance during a client's professional career, assessing whether a job in question fits the client's overall career plan. The manager's traditional role is *not*, however, to procure employment for the client. In some states, this is actually precluded by law. Under the laws of the states of California and New York, personal managers outside of the music business are specifically prohibited from finding jobs or "procuring employment" for clients.

- In the music business, recording artists, songwriters, and music producers *generally do not have agents*, so the personal manager serves both as the agent and the personal manager for a fee usually ranging from fifteen to twenty percent. California and New York laws require agency licenses for procuring employment within those states, and the music industry representative is specially carved out and exempted from some of those laws.

- In the publishing world, authors do not generally have personal managers, although they could if their careers required it.
- In the sports world, agents typically act both as the agent and the manager, which is one of main reasons these agents commission the player contract, as well as endorsement deals, and other agreements.

The Business Manager

At the appropriate time in your career, once you have achieved a certain level of financial success, you should consider hiring a professional business manager. Business managers are responsible for physically managing the financial aspects of your career and personal life, such as making sure you get paid the proper amounts, structuring the deal to get the more favorable tax treatment, or even paying your utility bills, mortgage, car notes, and taxes on time. They usually charge fees of either five percent of your gross income, monthly retainers, or an hourly rate fee structure. However, in the early stages of your career, presumably you would only need a personal manager or a talent agent on your team in order to start getting you professional jobs.

The Entertainment Lawyer

People frequently ask me, "When should I hire an entertainment attorney?"

I always answer this question the same way: *At the time you are presented with any contract (oral or written) or offer that potentially requires you to render services or sign away rights of any kind whatsoever.*

This can happen immediately when you get an agent or manager or once you're offered your first real job in the industry. The lawyer's role is to negotiate your deals on your behalf with regard to its terms and conditions as it concerns the actual formal legal agreement you'll enter upon taking the job. Your entertainment attorney also works closely with your talent agent and other representatives to structure a deal and to provide you with good strategic advice and counsel before you close a deal. This is where a lot of people make mistakes in the entertainment business. Many people believe that they only need an agent, arguing with some logic and reason, "Why should I give away *more* of my money when my agent is already taking so much? Besides, my agents can use their in-house attorneys to look over my contract."

With attorneys earning an additional five percent of a transaction or frequently in excess of $500 per hour in legal fees—depending on the fee arrangement—it is easy to see how a novice would be alarmed. Often they err on the side of what they perceive as smart frugality when it comes to hiring an entertainment attorney to join the team of advisors. Ultimately, such a seemingly cautious move today can prove to be an even more costly decision down the road.

For example: an actor books a starring role on a new television series and is beyond ecstatic. The champagne is on ice, and he or she can't wait to celebrate. But this is show *business* and the actor must still sign a contract to make the deal official.

It's important to note that, for this project, the studio used its in-house business and legal affairs attorneys to structure and negotiate the agreement on its behalf. Accordingly, when it's time to negotiate the deal, they come fully loaded with their best team of attorneys and studio deal term precedents. Generally, most studios or networks do not negotiate their deals through talent agents. They have sent the best, most qualified lawyers in the industry to represent them. This is in *no way* an attempt to malign agents who are of utmost importance to the process, but under such a scenario, why would you—with the biggest deal of your lifetime on the line—send your agent as your sole representative or their in-house counsel (whose loyalty is first to the agency) to negotiate your long-form agreements and your major deal terms? Despite the fact that many agents have law degrees, are extremely competent, and are there to look out for your best interests, negotiating long-form agreements is not their primary job function. In many circumstances, it's simply not the most prudent approach to take if you want to have the most effective team of advisors looking out for your sole interests.

Another common mistake people new to entertainment and sports success make is that when they do hire an attorney, it's not uncommon for them to hire someone who does not have the right entertainment or sports law expertise. No matter how much you trust him, your uncle who has a booming real estate law practice, or your cousin who just graduated from law school will just not do. It is vital that you hire an attorney who thoroughly understands the economics and legal issues pertaining to the type of transaction you are contemplating entering. Entertainment and sports law are highly specialized fields requiring unique skill sets, so hire an attorney who has, or has access to, good experience in the industry and legal precedents.

It is equally important to make sure your representatives do not have irreconcilable conflicts of interest that preclude you from getting the best deal. I recall the story of a young woman who was approached by a celebrity producer to host her own reality television show. For her, the show was the culmination of years of hard work in the business world. She was firmly established in her fifteen minutes, having successfully sustained her success beyond her first round of notable achievement. But our host was new to television, and this soon-to-be TV star needed an agent to represent her in the deal. The host asked the producer if he could recommend an agent. The producer shrewdly suggested that *his* agent represent her. Right away you can see the seeds of all kinds of potential problems being planted here. It is a potential conflict of interests because the agent cannot have an undivided loyalty to the artist and objectively evaluate the merits of the transaction on the artist's behalf. The agent in this scenario is often first and foremost concerned with protecting the economic interests of the producer with whom he shares a long-term relationship. Therefore, in the process of structuring the deal, the agent favored the interests of the producer at the expense of the show's host. To make matters worse—when the show host finally did hire her own attorney to review her contract, she used the agency's in-house attorney to negotiate her long-form agreement.

The artist had neither an independent agent nor an attorney representing her in the negotiations. When it was all said and done, she got a deal she later questioned. She had been so enamored with the excitement, glitz, and glamour of having a TV show that she didn't do any independent research. She was not prepared for success. In the end, she failed to properly handle the hardcore business aspects of her new opportunity by engaging her own dream team of advisors who would look out for her best interests above all else. The host later ended up severing ties with the agent and the producer, and then she filed a civil lawsuit against them, claiming millions of dollars in damages.

All of this may have been avoided if the artist had put the right team in place at the outset. If she had done her homework and proper research, she could have come to the table in a stronger and more confident position. While she may not have gotten a "perfect" deal—given that she was new to the business and an unproven television talent—she would have at least been treated fairly and with integrity. Her show was later cancelled and because of the close-knit and incestuous world of the entertainment business, her lawsuit against the network has since cost her valuable relationships and, quite possibly, new television opportunities. Despite numerous attempts, she has not worked in television since. Again, much of this debacle could have been prevented had she been prepared to handle her success when it arrived. Our TV host got her fifteen minutes of fame but didn't have the skills or the right team in place to take full advantage of the moment. Sadly, the entertainment and sports worlds are full of people who have made similar catastrophic errors.

When it comes to learning the ins and outs of the business, a question that frequently arises is— *When should I begin the process of acquiring the necessary information?* Needless to say, I'm a big advocate of starting early. In a society where children and parents may quickly find themselves manipulated by sports or entertainment representatives that prey on the young and uninformed, it is never too early to learn the fundamentals of the entertainment business. We live in a culture where many parents push hard for their kid to be the next sports, music, TV, or film star, which makes it important for both parents and children to understand how the business works. In fact, I think that it's paramount that parents and kids study the business together. When you consider the success of Dakota Fanning or the Olsen twins, it's not inconceivable that your child could grow up to become a multi-millionaire, so you want to be prepared.

In a world where more and more people are interested in entertainment and where blogging, easy access to digital video, and other new social media have made the everyday citizen a creator of intellectual property, you must understand the rules of the game. I encourage everyone wanting to venture into the world of entertainment to do some basic homework, including:

- Build a reliable network of good friends and advisors;
- Read insider books, the industry trades like *Variety*, *Hollywood Reporter*, and *Billboard*, along with other widely followed publications and blogs; and
- Attend seminars, and research, research, research. There is much too much at stake and too much information right at our fingertips to be uninformed.

I believe the ideal time to begin exposing children to the hardcore business aspects of the entertainment and sports industry is in high school when a child begins to seriously consider colleges and universities and the career path they might want to take. Great achievement in entertainment and sports often leads to sudden fame. Sudden fame, more than anything, creates access to people and situations that can help you build upon your success. When the door opens to your future, you must have a plan of action rather than simply living by the wind, osmosis, or a game of chance.

A good example is the popular TV show, *American Idol*. The show has proven that it could be your fifteen minutes. Whether you win or lose on the show, if you perform well enough, people recognize your genuine talent. If you are smart about the relationships you develop while on *Idol*, you might ultimately leverage your moment in the spotlight into something much bigger and better. Jennifer Hudson lost on *American Idol*, ranking fifth on her season. Judge Simon Cowell offered his honest opinion, pronouncing that her singing was, in so many words, terrible. But that didn't stop Hudson. Determined to parlay her national exposure into an even bigger arena, she got her big break two years later when she was cast in the film version of the hit Broadway musical *Dreamgirls*, before going on to win the Academy Award for best supporting actress. Hudson later landed a leading role in the ensemble film *The Secret Life of Bees* and a showy supporting role in the hit film *Sex In the City*, followed by an album in the fall of 2011.

Perhaps no person has demonstrated the ability to transcend adversity and negative publicity during their fifteen minutes and turn it into a positive like Vanessa Williams following her Miss America scandal. Williams has gone on to become a Grammy award-nominated recording artist and an award-winning successful actress, starring on Broadway and in several TV shows including ABC's *Ugly Betty*. Williams capitalized on her moment in the spotlight and ultimately trumped her very public failure by leveraging her genuine talents and depending on the loyalty of those in her inner circle and business associates who genuinely wanted her to succeed and survive all of the bad press.

Taking another look at maximizing the advantages of your big moment, let's assume you're an unknown actor and A-list director Michael Bay casts you in a summer blockbuster movie like *Transformers*. You're going to be featured in a movie watched by millions of people over the Fourth of July weekend. You have already identified this event as your fifteen minutes and understand that the decisions you make during this period will affect the direction of the rest of your life. It is critical at this juncture that you network with the directors, producers, writers, and other actors you meet in order to build alliances with powerful forces in the industry that will later allow you to capitalize on this opportunity and sustain your success.

Ultimately, it's all about ensuring career longevity. I always encourage people to think beyond the moment—beyond immediate gratification and success. I urge them to measure themselves by more than one or two experiences and to evaluate themselves by their sustained triumphs rather than their initial superficial perceptions of high achievement.

It's also necessary that you make a real effort to manage your finances by saving, investing wisely, and planning for the future. You should seek sound financial advice from a trusted professional within the financial community who can guide you toward solid appreciable assets such as stocks, bonds, and real estate, instead of depreciable items like cars, clothing, vacations, and other luxury goods which will only decline in value over time. Remember, if you are planning your future and living in the moment surrounded by empty assets that provide no financial return going forward, you only run the risk of financial challenges down the road. Anyone who is fortunate enough to hit it big financially in any profession should take these three simple pieces of advice to heart:

- Resist the urge to live for the moment.
- Avoid lavish, wasteful spending.
- Be willing to set boundaries with friends and family members who come to you for financial support.

Additionally, it's very important to think about where it is you want to be in the long run:

- Practice financial discipline.
- Resist the need to impress people, to compete with your peers by keeping score on material possessions. There's no need to keep up with the Joneses.
- Surround yourself with smart, loyal friends and business associates who share your values about personal finances and support your long-term objectives.

The reality is that we will all grow older and most of us will not be able to work at the same level that we worked at during our more youthful years. In maximizing your fifteen minutes, you should think about how you want to live as you age and plan for your future in terms of investments, healthcare insurance, and long-term care insurance.

In 2008, at the ripe old age of eighty-five, TV pitchman Ed McMahon received a lot of unwanted media attention because of his financial troubles, including facing imminent foreclosure on his Beverly Hills mansion. When explaining his dire money situation, McMahon, who reportedly had made millions of dollars over the course of his career, cited poor investments, excessive spending habits, and a broken neck, which had temporarily prevented him from working. One terrible aspect about McMahon's situation is that most people in America retire at age sixty-five. Unfortunately, it appears that had McMahon exercised good, long-term financial and retirement planning, he might have been able to absorb the consequences of not being able to work for a period. He arguably should never have had to worry about a job if he didn't want to at his advanced age. Luckily, McMahon was able to find a buyer for his home before the bank took possession of it. But with solid financial planning and by saving just a portion of the amount of money he made over the course of his career, he should have been living comfortably until the end of his life, enjoying the fruits of his hard labor.

Always remember—you are in a marathon and not a sprint.

It is key that you spend your days wisely, getting the absolute most of your fifteen minutes. *Pace yourself, plan for retirement, establish solid business relationships, and save at least some of the money you earned.* If you do this, you will be assured a substantially improved chance of achieving financial freedom and stability for the rest of your life.

Chapter 6

THE STATE OF THE INDUSTRY: DISRUPTIVE INNOVATIONS

"The quicker you let go of old cheese, the sooner you find new cheese." — Spencer Johnson, MD (from *Who Moved My Cheese?*)

To make the most of your fifteen minutes and move on to the sixteenth minute and beyond, you must examine your career and your industry in a global, macroeconomic context. Today, we live in a dynamic, interdependent digital world where changes are occurring at an unprecedented pace. Many of these changes are fueled by new developments in technology. However, disruptive innovations have created or eliminated entire industries or markets that have changed the way everybody conducts business today (e.g. replacing a brick and mortar print publication business with an Internet based digital publication). It's necessary for you to understand the current state of your industry in order to identify new trends, opportunities, and developments that will impact your business and your career going forward.

For several generations in America, life was all about going to school, getting a job, and working at that same job—often in the same position—for forty years, before retiring at the ripe age of sixty-five. Company loyalty was greatly valued and companies cherished their employees over the course of their lifetime. Employees were generally perceived as the most important asset to a company's success. In today's world, though, employee/company loyalty does not exist. We live in a competitive, global economy where technological advances and international competition have made it a common practice for companies to lay off thousands of employees and/or eliminate their benefits in an effort to cut costs, stay competitive, and boost shareholder value. Companies have stopped finding it necessary to offer employees guaranteed lifelong employment, top quality health benefits, and generous retirement packages. In our current economic reality, employees do not have a sense of stability or commitment in the workplace. In fact, it's no longer seen as taboo to leave a company and most people are expected to change jobs at least three times in a lifetime.[15]

Like many other industries, the entertainment industry

has been significantly affected by our changing times. Until recently, for several decades the television, film, and record industries held a monopoly on how all Americans spent leisure time or expressed creative talents. However, at a record pace in recent years, as several new forms of entertainment have become increasingly popular, the traditional television, film, and recording industries have been reduced to fighting for their very survival. For example: only a few years ago people were limited to watching television programs offered exclusively by the big three broadcast networks: ABC, CBS, and NBC. Because these networks were the only choices available to television audiences, they enjoyed a long-standing monopoly on viewership. But in today's television market, we have over two hundred choices in cable networks, seven choices in broadcast networks, and a plethora of choices in digital channels. In addition, the broadcast networks must not only compete with each other for viewers, but they must also contend with a host of entertainment and information options including the Internet, video games, DVDs, Netflix, video on demand, and mobile programming on smart phones and tablet devices. We have become a culture obsessed with our perpetually increasing, readily available entertainment choices. In our current environment, networks don't have the same unsophisticated audience pool they so easily controlled years ago. Modern-day audiences want their programming content to be accessible when, where, and how they want it—whether it's in their living room, streamed on their computer, on a mobile device, or as video on-demand. The modern viewer simply wants—and in many cases has—control.

The big three networks have also seen their viewership melt away as the industry has shifted to more niche-focused programming that targets specific viewers. The cable networks, streaming services like Hulu, and subscription providers like Netflix are new players that have been primarily responsible for the new treads in viewership. Historically, during the time of the big three broadcast networks, a top ten hit TV show routinely garnered eighty million or more viewers. Today, the number one show on the top ten ratings list is lucky to average fifteen million viewers. It's not that sixty-five million viewers have fallen out of love with TV, but now they can get their entertainment from sources other than the big three broadcast networks. The viewers are watching other channels such as Lifetime and Oxygen (which target women), Nickelodeon and the Disney Channel (which target kids), BET (which targets African Americans), Telemundo (which targets Latinos) or Spike TV (which targets males). The dizzying array of options available to viewers has created a fierce battle for advertising dollars as companies strategize to find the best platform to reach consumers.

This new paradigm shift has also occurred in the movie industry. Single screen theaters and drive-ins are now almost extinct as contemporary audiences flock to multiplexes where multiple screens can offer not only a number of different movies, but can also show the same popular film on multiple screens. Summer blockbuster franchise films like *Star Trek, Iron Man, the Fast and Furious,* or *the Transformers* are run on multiple screens at the same multiplex, and often on over four thousand screens nationwide. With so many screens available for a single film, the opening weekend has become a do-or-die scenario for movies. Films must connect with an unpredictable and easily distracted audience right out of the gate to avoid becoming labeled as the latest massive flop.

The music industry has been the most severely impacted by the paradigm shift to digital technology. From Naptser to iTunes, digital technology and consumer habits have changed every aspect of the record industry. The music business dominated by 8-tracks, vinyl albums, and CDs that many Americans grew up with no longer exists. For decades, a consumer was required to buy a physical copy of an album. Many consumers found themselves obliged to purchase the entire album even if they only wanted the one big hit song on the record. Today, with the advent of Internet downloads, single song sales dominate the record business. The industry has also been crippled by consumers who insist on music file sharing to feed their massive demand for free music.

As a result of these changes, audiences today are more discerning than ever before as they seek out what content best suits their specific tastes. The demand for more choices has resulted in increased production of entertainment programming. According to a Pricewaterhouse Coopers' report that presented its 2013-2017 Global Entertainment and Media Outlook, *"democratization of digital access to entertainment and media content is the key driver for industry growth and opportunity."* Pricewaterhouse predicts that global entertainment and media spending will rise from $1.6 trillion in 2012 to a record $2.2 trillion by 2017, with *"the U.S remaining the largest, most valuable territory in the world for all filmed entertainment."*

Although the digital revolution has changed the way in which we experience our entertainment, it remains one of the largest exported American products around the world. With the increased access to digital and streaming technology, there has been a paradigm shift that allows for more seats at the table. Many of the barriers to production and distribution have significantly decreased, which in turn has enabled more people to participate in both the creation and delivery of the product, as well as the consumer base. The changes we are experiencing today were on my mind as I graduated from law school and prepared to enter the legal profession in 1990. I paid attention when I heard some industry analysts suggest that in the future there would be five hundred television channels. Debate about the "information superhighway" began in the 1980s with books like *Megatrends* by John Naisbitt. Anticipating these changes early on, I believed that those who didn't take advantage of the information superhighway would either miss out or be late to accessing the new opportunities that were quickly developing in the entertainment industry.

Determined to take advantage of this emerging market, I planted the seeds of a career in law at Lord, Bissell and Brook, with a dream of someday actually having a full-time entertainment law practice.

The Lord Bissell headquarters in Chicago epitomized the classic "old boy network" mentality. Despite having a combined total of approximately three hundred lawyers in its offices across the country, I was one of only a few African Americans hired by the firm in its eighty-plus-year history. Although I never directly experienced any racial tension or hostility, I did notice that I was not invited to certain private networking functions, or asked by the partners to shoot hoops or hang out after work like some of my fellow junior associates. However, the firm did have several planned group events for the summer associates and I took full advantage of all of them. Because of the national firm network, the Los Angeles office of Lord Bissell had the feel of a small firm with major resources, and I definitely made friends and significant contacts within the firm that are still part of my network today.

After graduating from Georgetown, Lord Bissell offered me a full-time job as an associate. I was given a choice between working at the Chicago home office or going to the Los Angeles office. Between practicing law in the freezing winters of Chicago or practicing year-round in sunny LA, my choice was an easy one.

As an associate at Lord Bissell, I primarily practiced complex civil litigation and corporate transactions. My caseload usually involved multiple parties, with often millions and sometimes billions of dollars at stake. I enjoyed litigation because I was very comfortable walking and talking in front of people, including judges, and I enjoyed the elements of analyzing, preparing, and proving a case, along with the deal making and organizational aspects of practicing corporate transactional law. Between my litigation and corporate experiences, my hard work and good performances eventually paid off and the partners at the firm began to take notice of me.

After a full day of working on my regular caseload, I spent my evenings and weekends building a network in the entertainment industry. My plan was to build a solid base of good connections that would someday provide me the opportunity to sign my first entertainment clients. This strategy ultimately paid off and the first major entertainment client I signed was actress Kim Fields who had starred on the popular eighties TV series, *The Facts of Life*. Kim had been off the series for a few years when we met. At twenty-one, she was a college graduate with a degree in communications from Pepperdine University looking to re-launch her acting career. You could say she was attempting to secure her sixteenth minute of fame.

Kim and I really hit it off. We talked about strategy and how she could make the difficult transition from being a child star to an adult actress. Within a year of working together, Kim landed a lead role on the new Fox series, *Living Single*. As I negotiated her contract, in addition to using common sense, my legal expertise, and Kim's track record in television, I also sought guidance from a network of entertainment attorneys called the Black Entertainment and Sports Lawyers Association (BESLA), which I continue to be involved with to this day. Kim was pleased with the results and her show *Living Single* went on to run for five years.

My next core entertainment client was my long-time friend Rocky Carroll who had just completed his role on Broadway in *The Piano Lesson*. Charles Dutton, who had also starred in the play, was launching a sitcom for the new Fox Broadcast Network called *Roc*, and he asked Rocky to come to Los Angeles to join the cast. It proved to be an opportune time for Rocky and I to work together.

Although Rocky was already represented by a number of agents and a manager, we agreed that I would serve as his entertainment attorney and legal advisor. I later brought several more entertainment clients of all disciplines — actors, writers, producers, and directors—into the Lord Bissell firm. Some of them worked a lot and others were in the early development stages of their careers, but in my opinion all of them had the potential to make it big in the entertainment industry and I wanted to be their attorney when that day arrived for each client.

The unprecedented growth of the Fox Broadcast Network in the early nineties opened many doors and afforded me the opportunity to break into an industry that often can be unfriendly to outsiders. Fox was creating considerably more African American-themed content than the other three major networks combined. In the rapidly changing television industry, Fox was leading the way by delivering content to a niche audience. Headed by its president, Lucy Salhany, Fox created programming to appeal directly to African-American viewers as well as general-market viewers of urban content, using a strategy of building the network's base by targeting a niche audience to eventually compete with the big three broadcast networks.

Like so many great visionaries, Fox owner Rupert Murdoch was initially the laughing stock of the entertainment business world when he set out to create a fourth network.

But Murdoch would have the last laugh when Fox Network's strategy proved to be right. Fox soon learned that under-served African-American audiences were more brand loyal to watching African American actors on any television network where they saw themselves represented. This was the opposite viewing habit of the main stream general-market audience who typically inherited their viewing patterns by being brand loyal to one of the three major networks: CBS, ABC, or NBC. As a result, it was much more difficult to get general-market viewers to switch over to watching the new Fox network.

In the nearly impenetrable world of Hollywood, the Fox shows opened doors for many African-American actors, writers, directors, producers, production crews, and executives, providing game-changing access to many new television industry opportunities.

Working with my five most successful entertainment clients underscored the business philosophy I had been developing and brought me to an important conclusion: *Building and sustaining careers centers on transitioning to the next level.*

My clients were all smart with good credentials and connections, and I knew I could set myself apart from their other advisors and representatives by encouraging them to plan beyond their present success by finding new opportunities outside the box. If I could help them get to the sixteenth minute in their careers, I believed I would naturally advance my career as well.

My initial plan was to become a partner at Lord Bissell—an ambition that seemed quite probable, as my superiors were impressed with my ability to attract clients and my overall performance at the firm. I got along and worked well with my colleagues and staff in the office and I was consistently ranked as one of the top associates with high billable hours. By most standards, I was frequently told I met the criterion to become a partner some day. But in spite of my solid contributions to the firm and the very real prospect of achieving partner status, the firm did not seriously expect me to follow through with my plans to create an entertainment practice and become a legitimate entertainment attorney. Although I had a lot of support, I suspected there were some people who were less than enthusiastic to see me rise and simply weren't ready to move as a firm to the next level. As a result, my entertainment practice eventually outgrew the confines of the expertise at the firm and I was left with a dilemma—either stay at Lord Bissell with its limited vision of the future, or leave the firm and try to associate with attorneys who had more entertainment experience and resources that would allow me to grow my practice.

After seriously pondering the issues, analyzing my options, and accessing the risk of failure, I decided that although I was eternally grateful for the five years of experience and training that had actually contributed to making me a better dealmaker while at Lord Bissell, it was time for me to move on.

Based on the excellent training I received at Lord Bissell and my unwavering commitment to practicing full-time entertainment law, I felt ready for the next level of my life and I was looking forward to making entertainment law my primary focus. After leaving the firm, I was hired by a boutique entertainment law firm in Beverly Hills. Working mainly on talent deals for television, motion pictures, and licensing opportunities, I brought my five major clients with me to the new firm. From the beginning, everything at my new firm was great. I drafted countless contracts, billed more hours in six months than I had in one year at Lord Bissell, and was working so hard that I even caught pneumonia a couple of times. Believe it or not, I was incredibly happy at that moment just to be actually practicing full-time entertainment law and fulfilling my dream. However, I often questioned whether all the stressful hours and turning over all the revenue generated by my own clients was worth the modest salary I was obliged to accept as I was "paying my dues to get into the industry." But the promise from the partners that I would be treated fairly and well-compensated at bonus time motivated me to keep going.

Bonus day arrived—a day I shall never forget for as long as I live. I can still remember my excitement when my boss took me to lunch at the Mandarin restaurant in Beverly Hills. He extolled my virtues, telling me how "great" I was doing, just how "great" I was, and going so far to say that if I kept performing so well, one day I'd be a "great" lawyer. I remember thinking, "Great! This bonus check is going to be *good!*" Finally, my boss slid the check over to me. I looked down at the figure. I checked the zeros again. Then I checked my pulse. Then I checked his eyes and my heart sank. I had expected a generous or at least respectable check that would reflect the work I had put in on behalf of their clients or, at the very least, the fees collected by the firm from the clients that I brought into the firm. But the check lying on the table in front of me was a mere fraction of what my boss—who knew exactly how many hours I had billed and how much client fees were collected as a result of my work—should have offered. He knew very well I had student loans to repay and that I needed those cost-of-living funds to survive in Los Angeles as a struggling young attorney who was just trying to keep his head above water.

Recovering from my initial disappointment, I decided it was time for me to part ways with the firm. It was definitely time for me to focus on myself and count on my own abilities. I finally asked myself—*Why give all of my time, energy, intelligence, and resources to people who do not respect or value me when I could apply my energy to build a home for myself?*

My first concern was to have my five major clients come with me. I was scared to death because up until that point I had only worked for other firms with other people's names on the shingle. My mind was racing: "What if the clients were only happy with me because I was backed by a well-established and successful firm?" Or worse: "What if they did not believe I could do it by myself?" Without my clients, I feared I had nothing and all of my hard work with them up to that point would be sacrificed. That said, I strongly believed I had to take the risk regardless of which way their loyalties fell.

To my great relief, all of my clients said, "Wherever you are, we're with you." Their support was an amazing testament to their confidence and respect for my abilities. With my clients on board, I knew I could manage my lifestyle and personal choices in a way that would be both gratifying and dignified. I knew I could serve my clients even better than before. I often felt like the firm's unofficial mission statement was to teach the associates that the clients were not the people who matter most. For the partners' purposes it was the agents and managers who really counted. "Clients come and go," they'd say, "so don't get too attached to them." It was difficult for me to conclude that they did not believe in investing in individual clients for the long-term but in focusing on the people who could send them more business in the future. In my opinion, these "old school" partners believed in taking big fees from the clients while you can and keeping it going as long as you can. There was nothing about the concept of the sixteenth minute in their mission. The firm's philosophy put me in an ethical dilemma from the very beginning. As a performer, I understood the lonely feeling of not having an advocate who has your back, but as a lawyer I was trained at Lord Bissell to believe that my responsibility, loyalty to, and respect for my clients reigned supreme. Thankfully, Georgetown University Law Center and Lord Bissell provided me with a good education and foundation in how to practice law with ethics and character.

On January 31, 1996, I left the boutique firm in Beverly Hills and February 1, 1996, was the first official day I opened my *own* doors and hung up my *own* shingle as Darrell D. Miller, A Professional Law Corporation. From that moment on, I was determined to run my practice in a way that would reflect my own values as an attorney and as a person. I have never looked back. Ultimately, I had taken a gamble on myself that would allow me to take advantage of the many great changes taking place in the entertainment industry.

Chapter 7

THE SEVEN STREAMS OF INCOME THEORY

"The toughest thing about success is that you've got to keep on being a success."
—Irving Berlin

In the mid-1990s, while I was looking for a way to distinguish myself and grow my law practice, I began developing a business strategy. I concluded that if you identify a brand, leverage that brand across multiple distribution platforms, and have an effective transition plan, you could significantly improve the chances of sustaining success. From that point on, I dedicated myself to helping individuals and companies develop multiple streams of income as a winning strategy for my business model.

Irving Berlin is considered to be one of the greatest songwriters in American history. Born in 1888, he achieved his first fifteen minutes of fame and became world famous by the age of twenty-three after writing his first international hit song, "Alexander's Ragtime Band." He went on to compose hundreds of songs, nineteen Broadway shows, and eighteen Hollywood films. Irving Berlin is a prime example of an artist who, by his words and actions, successfully leveraged his fifteen minutes of fame by generating multiple streams of income as a key to sustaining his success.

Defining Your Brand

Starting my own law practice was the equivalent of establishing my own brand. When I put my name out on that proverbial shingle on February 1, 1996, and opened the doors to my own law firm, I was essentially asking people to see me as an expert in my area of practice. I was also asking potential clients to trust that my name and services would be of the highest quality and would add value to their projects. Once I was able to successfully establish my brand with a solid client base, I was in the position to leverage my skills into working with many successful celebrity clients. In time, I was able to build a successful law practice by monetizing my brand.

This strategy applies to actors, musicians, athletes, executives, business owners, and anyone else who has a recognizable brand. Once your name has been recognized by the public or key influencers, is associated with good quality, and establishes you as the go-to-expert or celebrity in your field, you have the foundation for creating multiple streams of income through leveraging your brand. The challenge then becomes to actually cross-promote or leverage your brand into something long lasting that turns into a meaningful income stream.

The business of marketing and brand management is the process of learning how to identify, understand, and target an audience, then getting that audience to experience you again and again on various distribution platforms in traditional media or in the on-demand environment of social media.

Cross-promotion is the means by which a brand can be leveraged to reach new audiences and new markets. In these modern times, you can begin to track your audience and create a database that will allow you to market your brand directly to your audience just as large companies do with their branded products and services. In the past, you needed to have your brand or product distributed by a mass-distribution company in order to reach a large audience, but now the Internet has become the great equalizer that allows individuals or small business to reach audiences on a mass scale.

Consumers who are brand loyal can help a brand thrive in new markets. Most notable is the way celebrity merchandising and endorsement deals are used to sell everything from toothpaste to expensive cars. Major Hollywood studios and record companies are good examples of how brands are traditionally used to cross-promote movies, broadcast television, and the next big multi-platinum music artist. A Hollywood motion picture blockbuster like *Spider-Man* could easily generate merchandising opportunities in the form of *Spider-Man* toys at McDonalds, bed linen at Target and Wal-Mart, clothing at J.C. Penney, candy at 7 Eleven, and even gym shoes at Footlocker—not to mention the *Spider-Man* DVD, comic books, personal appearances, tours, and soundtracks. Each element of these properties has the potential to become an additional income stream for the studio. For many studio franchise films, these ancillary revenues often exceed box office revenues for the movie. A number of hit television shows go on to generate hundreds of millions of dollars in syndication just as hit songs enable music artists and record companies to generate millions in live tours, merchandising, and publishing revenues.

People should think of themselves as a brand that can be cross-promoted in much the same way studio films, television shows, and hit records are leveraged. If you establish yourself as a brand, your audience will follow because of their loyalty, familiarity, and commitment to you. The Internet has made this completely possible today in ways that never existed before. And because you can now more effectively than ever cross-promote your brand, you are ultimately in the position to monetize that relationship into multiple income streams just as big corporations do.

Depending on your skills and interests, cross-promotional opportunities can be boundless. In the entertainment industry, an actor can leverage their talents into writing, directing, or producing. The actor can even set up a production company, act as a financier, or offer their social media following as a distribution platform for a fee. The roles below come with the potential to generate seven streams of income without even stretching too far beyond the actor's core talent:

1. Actor
2. Writer
3. Director
4. Producer
5. Production Company Owner
6. Financier
7. Distributor

When selling books, an author can cross-promote books on CDs and DVDs, appear at speaking engagements, and conduct writing workshops. Adjunct professorships at local colleges and universities also provide authors an opportunity to become a part of a vibrant academic community and build an audience for their work. The theory is that people who enjoy your books might also enjoy your work in other media and enjoy you as a personality.

The following list presents seven potential streams of income without straying too far from a writer's basic skills:

1. Book Writer
2. CDs/DVDs
3. Personal Appearances
4. Workshops
5. Teaching
6. Television/Film Writer
7. Speech Writer

The Seven Streams of Income theory applies to other professions as well, such as business executives:

1. Primary Job
2. Stock Portfolio
3. Real Estate Investments
4. Books
5. Personal Appearances
6. Ownership in one business
7. Ownership in a second business

There are no magic seven streams of income that everybody must have. Each person should have their own list of seven.

Your seven streams should first start with your main job or skill. Then you should build the other six streams around your core business or profession. Like many wealthy Americans, creating income streams from investing in stock, businesses, and real estate are good ideas to consider including on your list. Most creative or successful people I meet actually have far more than seven different ideas or opportunities to generate income. I have had clients who successfully managed as many as twenty different income streams between their job and investments. However, I have found that when most people are starting out, they are often overwhelmed with their options and frequently get mentally blocked on how to move forward. Unfortunately, this limits their ability to actually put the necessary action plans in place behind their good ideas.

Actors and other creative people often come to my office with a million ideas and no strategic plan to execute them. That's where my business strategy of seven streams of income can be most helpful. In many cases, it helps people focus on their primary business opportunities and develop a serious plan to build and sustain multiple income streams.

Although the concept of cross-promotion is hardly new, we live in a society that is inherently risk-averse. Nowhere has this been more apparent than in the entertainment business where the idea of brand extension and cross-promotion for artists has not always been embraced. In fact, an anti-cross-promotion attitude was pervasive throughout the industry when I came to Los Angeles in the late 1980s. There was a rather narrow view of the business—even within the larger talent agencies with film, television, theater, and literary divisions—that singers do not act, film actors do not work in television, actors do not write, authors do not sing, and so on and so on. Everyone was pigeonholed into doing the one thing for which they were primarily known. They were severely limited by the concept that only what worked in the past will work in the future. Agencies did not want to sacrifice the success they had already garnered by placing their artists in unproven venues. There was no vision for new possibilities.

The limited perspective in the industry regarding cross-promotion reflected the general mindset of the country at the time. It was in keeping with the old company/employee loyalty position that locked the employee into doing just one thing for their entire life—*Go to school. Get a job. Work at that job for several years. Get your gold watch. Retire.* But I believed the old paradigm was in the process of shifting for the average person, and it was definitely shifting even more rapidly for entertainers. Strongly believing there were going to be many entertainment choices for consumers in the near future, I adopted the idea of cross-promotion and began to develop and expand the concept of branding. I reasoned that the best way to get an audience to choose your product would be by offering them a brand they already knew and trusted.

The key to getting into the entertainment business in the future depends on establishing brands and getting audiences to stay with those brands across different media outlets or distribution platforms.

While developing my concept of the business and working with my first clients in my own law firm, we attempted to stay ahead of the curve. For example, most people know Kim Fields as an actress, but very few people know that she is of the few African-American women to be admitted into the Director's Guild of America (DGA), a union organization that represents professional directors in the film and television industries. It was actually very cool to see Kim's evolution to the director's chair when we pushed to get her qualified for DGA membership while she directed episodes of *Living Single*.

Kim did not stop there. Her thought was, "If I can be in the DGA, I can start producing and writing as well." So Kim began creating her own content by writing scripts. Eventually she started her own production company called Mogul Entertainment.

Today, audiences have become very accustomed to seeing their favorite artists do a wide array of things, from acting to designing furniture. Given the rapid changes in the entertainment business, cross-promotion has become an important tool for entertainers to have sustainable success. In addition, the power has shifted from the small group of giant companies that controlled the few big pipelines of distribution, to the individual artists or celebrity of today who can reach their most brand loyal consumers directly through their social media platforms.

By any standard, Oprah Winfrey is the quintessential cross-promoter. She has successfully used her fame and fortune established by her daytime talk show to venture into movies, a television network, production company, acting, developing new talent like Dr. Phil and Dr. Oz, a national magazine, a major Broadway production, an influential book club, and more recently into politics. She even earned an Academy Award nomination for her role in the 1985 film *The Color Purple*. It certainly seems that everything Oprah puts her name on turns to gold.

Madonna also knows the all-reaching power of her name. She is a brilliant cross-promoter and brander, having leveraged her music into blockbuster tours, books, films, licensing, and merchandising. As reported by *Billboard*, her reported ten-year, $120 million deal with Live Nation Inc. covers literally everything her show will generate, from live performance to DVDs and merchandise.

In the world of sports, former NBA great Irving "Magic" Johnson has taken his persona earned on the basketball court to the corner office. Johnson's business interests have spanned everything from the ownership of sports franchises to licensing deals with movie theaters, restaurants, Starbucks coffee shops and ownership in the Los Angeles Dodgers. Johnson, wisely builds on his brand by using the "all-access pass" his name provides to open doors that otherwise might not be open to other entrepreneurs.

Johnson has also developed a direct relationship with his fan base. Magic Johnson Enterprises thrives under the powerful mantra: *We are the communities we serve.* This maxim generates income and opportunities to sustain his long-term success. In addition, he has used his influence to advance the field of medicine and to increase public awareness about HIV/AIDS. Johnson also gives back generously to his local community and to society worldwide through his philanthropic activities.

When evaluating the potential of your brand, it's important that you consider all of your personal attributes and accomplishments. During my career, I've had the opportunity to work with a few actresses and actors who enjoyed great success in their past by starring in or playing memorable roles in hit films and television shows. A few of these actors even received Academy or Emmy Award nominations for their work. However, I began to notice a trend for actors when their careers began slowing to a standstill. Nothing was really working for them and the role offers slowed down considerably. Some of them often complained, "I have not had a hit. I'm no longer on top. It's all over." I was instrumental in changing that negative attitude and convinced these artists that their fans and certain key influencers saw them differently.

I was confident they still had a viable brand which they had built over the years and which could be tapped into without any major studio or network giving them the green light. I explained to them that hit movies and television shows that generated audiences in the range of forty to fifty million people in America, also had millions of dedicated fans that had not forgotten their face and name. In fact, these loyal fans were probably waiting for their return to the big or small screen and were more than willing to trust their brands to deliver other high quality products and services. The inspiration that these actors had given to their film and TV audiences could potentially carry them over into other areas. If the fans loved the actor or actress on screen, they would likely love to see them in other businesses as well. To that end, I encouraged many of these actors to write books, develop merchandising businesses, endorse products, write, direct, produce or find some other way to identify and communicate with their fan base. This would get their creative juices flowing and monetize their brand extensions. I also encouraged them to learn the basics of social media and to then use that platform as their own television network or distribution portal to reach their target audience.

Many of these artists have gone on to start successful businesses, write books, and pursue a variety of opportunities that were never on their radar before they started thinking differently about how to leverage their brands.

Tyler Perry has been an absolute wizard at exploiting his brand and his database of consumers for cross-promotion. The playwright and actor—turned film producer/director/ television producer/author—has mastered the art of going directly to his audience. Perry first demonstrated a unique ability to target African-American theatergoers, movie lovers, television audiences, and readers with his family-themed, faith-based content that has transcended the original target audience and attracted other mass-market groups. According to Box Office Mojo, Perry's lifetime domestic box office gross of his films total $696 million dollars. According to *Variety*, he has sold 25 million DVDs. These impressive stats clearly demonstrate the viability of Perry's brand. He has built an empire based upon his ability to provide a consistent product to his audience that is firmly rooted in black family relationships.

Because he has mastered the management of the fan database of his niche, Perry has the ability to largely predict his audience. His movies, plays, books, and television show, *The House of Payne*, on TBS, are all marketed through his website. The result is an ongoing dialogue with the community of people who consume his products; he is always connected to his fan base in the digital environment. Perry's audience literally knows everything he's going to do and where to find it. The success of a project is almost instantaneous because he is able to take advantage of his already established brand loyalty.

In today's market, everybody has the capacity to use the Internet to effectively build brands and target consumers. A properly serviced website with a fan club base allows you to do the same things a studio does without the filter of anyone else. Everybody has the potential to exploit the various platforms available for their intellectual property. Why should someone else collect the checks on all of those various income streams you have worked so hard to produce?

Establish your brand, learn how to effectively cross-promote it, and the world will be yours.

Why Seven Income Streams?

After researching wealth in America during the nineties, I discovered that the average wealthy person in America has at least seven streams of income that support their financial stability. I also learned that many of these wealthy people typically maintain a job as an executive or CEO. In addition, they have real estate holdings and an investment portfolio. They also frequently invest in or start multiple businesses. If they lost their primary job, or if their stock portfolio took a loss, or if a business failed, they still had six other streams of revenue to rely on. Everybody wants to be like the rich, but few people who are not rich actually take the time to understand and examine the characteristics of rich people. At the conclusion of my research, I decided that developing multiple income streams is the best way to sustain yourself and your lifestyle over the course of your life. It will enable you to avoid the stress of being dependent on a single paycheck from a single source.

In order to assure long-term economic stability, it's important to have stock portfolios, real estate, and other business investments as a significant component of your strategy for protecting yourself from the ongoing consolidation and downsizing that has become an omnipresent part of our global economy. In other words, *diversification of your business ventures is one key to getting to your sixteenth minute of fame.*

The question that you should ask yourself is: *"What happens when my movie is over, my television show is off the air, or my record stops selling? Will I lose everything?"* The answer is: *"Not likely if you cross-promote your brand to create at least seven distinct income streams."*

Just as it would not be prudent to put all of your money in one stock, it would not be a sign of good career planning to put all of your skills into one job. The same concept applies to the entertainment industry—diversify your talent, apply it to other mediums and products, and you should have far less to worry about. Cushioned by your multiple income streams, you will be able to ride out the inevitable highs and lows of the industry.

I tell my clients to sit down and create a list of their seven possible income streams (see the list below on Appendix A). When I pose that question, most people find that they haven't organized their thoughts enough to really know what their seven priorities or possibilities are. In our second meeting, I begin to compile the list, and if the client can think of three items, then that's where we start. We can then identify more income streams that will work synergistically with the first three we have already established.

When coming up with your own particular income streams, it's best to begin with areas that are somewhat related. Trying to set up a car dealership or a dry cleaning business while recording music and making movies is probably not the smartest place to start. Because of the dissimilar natures of those business endeavors, you might find that each demands too much separate time and attention, ultimately causing a drain on valuable time and resources needed elsewhere. This would render those income streams less effective overall than if you worked on more complimentary business ventures such as a clothing line and a boutique.

My recommendations regarding multiple income streams to clients are aligned with my previous discussion of cross-promotion earlier in the chapter. If you are a singer, for example, my suggestions for developing other complimentary income streams would be:

1. Consider pursuing roles in movies and television;
2. Write a book or a book series;
3. Get a voiceover agent to book you jobs;
4. Record DVDs or other visual recorded products;
5. Consider launching a clothing line so your fans can dress like you;
6. If entertaining at home is your specialty, you might pursue a line of high-end china like Rachael Ray or other merchandizing items;
7. Never forget about stocks and real estate investments based on your risk tolerance.

These various income streams can operate in conjunction with, or sometimes depart from, your main source of income. Whatever you decide, it's important to understand that crossing into new territories requires solid preparation. If you're ill equipped, jumping into something unfamiliar can be more costly than had you never diversified at all. Oftentimes the rules and skill sets required for one field do not easily apply to another. You must do your research and learn what is required in the new environment.

Some entertainers—particularly certain rock and hip-hop stars who are notorious for being late, unprofessional, and irresponsible, have become infamous for making bad transitions into other industries in failed attempts to diversify. Indulgent record company executives and managers often cover up their antics, which only serves to aid in their bad behavior. But when these rappers take their bad attitudes and outlandish—sometimes even criminal activities—into the world of film or television where millions of dollars are at stake, the results will be more likely to severely set their careers back rather than propel them forward.

Once the word is out in the industry about their poor work ethic or personality issues, no producer, director, studio, or network will want to work with them. The stakes are far too high to take a chance on a person who could prove to be a major liability to the production.

As you move forward in your career, it's important that you survey the terrain and be alert for new and exciting ways to make money while you work within your main profession. Keep your eyes, your ears, and your options open, and you will be positioned to assure financial stability for a lifetime.

Know Your Exit Strategy

Once you have identified your seven streams of income, how much income you want to make with each stream, and the order in which you plan to achieve those streams, you must then apply a strategy of execution to transition from your present position to the next. Your exit strategy is not a "quit" strategy, but rather a method of determining at what point you have achieved enough in your current profession or discipline to leverage that success and flow into your next area of interest.

But what if you never want to exit? I can only echo author Spencer Johnson's sage wisdom: *"The quicker you let go of old cheese, the sooner you find new cheese."*

Johnson's wonderful little book tells the story of two mice and two little people living in a maze who discover one day that their normally reliable cheese supply is no longer fresh and, even worse, it's diminishing rapidly. They all react in different ways, but the ultimate result is the same: they all end up doing absolutely nothing. They just wait and hope that a new cheese supply will one day miraculously appear, but of course it doesn't. Only the little mouse that overcomes his fear and complacency is able to search the maze and find a fresh supply of cheese. Just like the plan many of our parents followed, as long as things seem to stay the same and it pays to continue doing what you've always done, you'll be content to stay in place. But if your cheese turns old and moldy while everybody around you is eating tasty new cheese, you might be motivated to come up with another game plan to get some new cheese. Blind resistance to change and a stubborn attitude could leave you wasting away in a dead career or business that is no longer a bright and shining star. It's time for you to move on. In another scenario, you don't want to be caught with a market turning downward or a business opportunity going away before you've had a chance to leverage the success. Be very aware when you've reached that plateau. You must always prepare an exit strategy for your career plan.

The exit strategy is not a new concept. It's broadly taught in MBA programs across America and is a core tenant of traditional business philosophy. In short, the exit strategy is the planned exit of an owner from their business.

I know it can seem like an odd thing to plan when you're just starting out, but most business experts agree that planning how you exit your business is just as important as how you start it—and is often more complicated. A well thought-out exit strategy will ensure you end your involvement in an enterprise with as little disruption to the business operations as possible. Without that crucial strategy, an individual or organization could end up damaging the business and jeopardizing the entity's ability to maintain and increase its optimal performance. An exit strategy doesn't just apply to flipping a business and selling it. It can also apply to your options as you continue to grow the business by expanding internationally or offering new product lines. The key about exit strategies is that they intentionally plan for change.

It's inevitable that your present career as you know it will end. The average life cycle of a sports or entertainment figure's career is three to five years. The average life cycle of a business professional is probably five to seven years. Your exit may be forced upon you or may be self-imposed. But it *will* happen. We are no longer in the America that existed for our parents. For most people, contemporary life has changed and expanded the possibilities of their future dramatically.

You exit one level to move to the next. You exit one profession to move to another. Or you may even exit from one fifteen-minute experience to move to a brand new fifteen minutes. Given those circumstances, an exit strategy is paramount. When moving on to the next phase of their careers, a lot of actors become directors, producers, or writers. These disciplines provide very natural and very successful transitions. On the business front, it's even possible that these jobs could all be handled within the same contract of a particular project.

Nevertheless, they are four separate and distinct jobs and four separate and distinct paychecks. It is an excellent way to establish your presence in the industry, build upon your craft, and create future opportunities versus just being an actor on the payroll.

I am passionate about helping my clients build bridges between multiple streams of income. I have had too many clients come to me and tell me that they blew their first million dollars. I have also watched too many first generational rich clients make unwise decisions after they reach extraordinary levels of momentary wealth and fame. Usually, it's because they lived a lifestyle in a naïve expectation that their good fortune would continue forever. If the average life expectancy is seventy years, and success at its pinnacle for most artists is three to five years, you can't justify living those three to five years as if they will never end. It's just not wise. You typically have twenty to thirty more years to provide for. You want to be prepared to live them well and in comfort.

As you consider your exit strategy, several questions will come up:

- When your fifteen minutes are over, what are you going to do?
- How do you sustain your fulfillment?
- How do you maintain your excitement?
- How do you keep your forward thinking motivation?
- Can you take your brand and apply it to different projects that generate multiple income streams?

The answers to these questions are positive and forward thinking:

- *You can*—if you correctly identify your fifteen minutes of fame and make the right decisions while you're enjoying those fifteen minutes.
- *You can*—if you spend an equal amount of time planning on *staying successful* as you do trying to *become successful.*

- *You can*—if you live for the sixteenth minute and beyond.
- *You can*—if you always remember: *"It's not where you are; it's where you are going...."*

AFTERWORD

"That some achieve great success, is proof to all that others can achieve it as well." —Abraham Lincoln

It's essential to expect great things to happen in your life. As Andy Warhol predicted, we will all get our fifteen minutes. And under that premise, your life must focus on *expecting, anticipating, and planning for your success.*

Everything I do in my life is in preparation for a great moment to begin. I believe something big is always on the horizon. I've learned from experience that it's a healthy point of view and a positive way to live life—wake up each day and look forward to what extraordinary thing might happen next.

Now it's your time to start your plan, or organize and focus your streams of income. To that end, I encourage you to focus, build your team, and execute your strategic plan for getting to your sixteenth minute. I've created a chart (see Appendix A) that will assist you as you begin to develop your strategic plan. Using the strategies I outlined in Chapter 7, write down your first seven streams of income. Once you have carefully completed the chart, you can begin the journey of securing your sixteenth minute. Each and every time you achieve a new dream, you should always ask yourself:

- *Question: "What do I do now?"*
- *Answer: Have a plan for maintaining my success beyond fifteen minutes of fame.*
- *Question: What are the first five phone calls that I should make to get help with sustaining my fame and fortune?*
- *Answer: Among your list, you might include (1) a mentor or advisor; (2) a good financial planner or accountant; (3) a good attorney; (4) a business or life coach; and (5) a good friend who can help you stay focused on your long-term plan of reaching the sixteenth minute of fame and not your immediate appearance of success.*
- *Question: What kind of team do I need to build my success to the next level?*
- *Answer: This will depend on your actual streams of income listed on your Chart, but the first five calls listed above are always a good place to start.*

- *Question: How can I insure that I am around for my sixteenth minute of fame?*
- *Answer: Never give up on your plan. And whatever you do, don't live in the past by putting all of your eggs in one basket. You cannot succeed in the twenty-first century by using twentieth century strategies.*

And finally, always remember: *Every day you prepare for your moment you can be on your way to your 16th Minute of Fame.*

APPENDIX

List your first seven streams of revenue in order of priority. If you need help, refer to the subsection entitled "Why Seven Revenue Streams?" in Chapter Seven.

1. _____

2. _____

3. _____

4. _____

5. _____

6. _____

7. _____

ENDNOTES

1. Holy Bible, New International Version by Biblica, Inc.

2. People.com, originally published "Redd Foxx Exits, Laughing" By Mark Goodman.

3. "The Ticket to Easy Street? The Financial Consequences of Winning the Lottery" by Scott Hankins of University of Kentucky, Mark Hoekstra of University of Pittsburgh—Department of Economics and Paige Marta Skiba of Vanderbilt Law School, Published in the *Vanderbilt Law and Economics Research Paper No. 10-12*, March 26, 2010.

4. "How (and Why) Athletes Go Broke" by Pablo S. Torre, *Sports Illustrated* Magazine Article, March 23, 2009.

5. "How (and Why) Athletes Go Broke" by Pablo S. Torre, *Sports Illustrated* Magazine Article, March 23, 2009.

6. Scoreboards—"Top 7 NFL Stars to Go Bankrupt", Electro-Mech Scoreboard Company, August 1, 2009.

7. Examiner.com. By Gordon Duncan. Published on August 31, 2011.

8. "10 Star Athletes Who Excelled at Losing Millions" by Ron Dicker, DailyFinance.com, September 19, 2011.

9. "10 Star Athletes Who Excelled at Losing Millions" by Ron Dicker, DailyFinance.com, September 19, 2011.

10. "Dues for Middle-Class SAG Actors, Most Dual Cardholders Would Decrease in Merger (Analysis)" by Jonathan Handel, *The Hollywood Reporter*, Hollywoodreporter.com. March 3, 2012.

11. Remarks by Harry Belafonte to the Veterans of the Lincoln Brigade/Abraham Lincoln Brigade Archives and friends celebrating the 60th anniversary of the Abraham Lincoln Brigade's arrival in Spain. The event was held at Boro of Manhattan Community College, 199 Chambers St at West St, New York City, on Sunday, April 27, 1997, at 2:00pm.

12. Excerpt from Testimony of Paul Robeson before Congress, House, Committee on Un-American Activities, Investigation of the Unauthorized Use of U.S. Passports, 84th Congress, Part 3, June 12, 1956.

13. English Standard Version of the Bible by Good News Publishers.

14. "Financial Windfall" Publication by National Endowment for Financial Education, 2001 (revised 2004).

15. "Number of Jobs Held, Labor Market Activity, and Earnings Growth Among the Youngest Baby Boomers: Results From a Longitudinal Survey", Bureau of Labor Statistics, United States Department of Labor, September 2010.

ACKNOWLEDGEMENTS

This book has been a long time coming. It took a backseat for many years to my unwavering dedication to serving the needs of my family, clients, and real friends. Throughout the process of writing this book, there were several people who gave me the support, encouragement, and ultimate push to see this project through for the benefit of all of those people who might be changed by my message. To that end, I want to acknowledge the following family members, friends, clients and colleagues, and say a sincere thank you for helping me deliver this book to readers who want to reach their sixteenth minute of fame:

Shannon J. Miller	Reva Miller
Angel Miller	Mark Miller
Douglas Miller, Jr.	Susie Louiso
Taylor J. Suero	Jack Louiso
Kent Ewing	Rocky Carroll
Amari Miller	Ethan Tucker

Belinda Wilkins

Jewel White

Johan Suero

Blair Underwood

Angela Bassett

Courtney B. Vance

Bishop TD Jakes

Daymond John

Chris Robinson

Jessy Terrero

George Alexander

Stella Anderson

David DiCristofaro

Donna Brazile

Terrence Jenkins

Lynnie Schwartz

Charles D. King

Paula White

George C. Fraser

Kyle D. Bowser

David Dunham

Lynne Scott

Andre Benjamin

Chris Bridges

Jeff Dixon

Chaka Zulu

Janie Schwartz

Nancy Schwartz

Charles Lee

Shaun Robinson

Bill Duke

Norman Aladjem

David White

ABOUT THE AUTHOR

 Darrell Miller, managing partner of Fox Rothschild LLP's Los Angeles offices and chair of the firm's Entertainment Law Department, has been at the forefront of the transformation taking place in the entertainment industry, helping stars capitalize on their brands as a result of the emergence of new delivery platforms and media outlets.

With over 20 years of experience in entertainment law, he has been acknowledged as a trailblazer among Hollywood entertainment lawyers with such accolades as *The Hollywood Reporter* including him in its 2013 list of the Top 100 Entertainment Power Lawyers in America, Variety identifying him as one of the most important Hollywood dealmakers in the *Dealmakers Impact Report* 2013, the National Bar Association naming him the 2012 Entertainment Lawyer of the Year, and by consistently appearing in *Black Enterprise Magazine*'s Top 50 Showbiz Players. He was inducted in the Black Entertainment & Sports Lawyers Association's Hall of Fame in 2007 and honored by the Foundation for Second Chances with its 2011 Service in Entertainment Leadership Award for his unwavering professional reputation as an entertainment attorney as well as for his philanthropic involvement with arts institutions.

Mr. Miller's clients include Grammy-winning, Golden Globe-nominated and Academy Award-nominated stars as well as companies and executives involved with development, production, distribution and marketing of entertainment products and services. He has also served as special counsel for major corporations doing business with the entertainment industry.

Darrell serves on the Board of Directors for the Music Center in Los Angeles, the Pasadena Playhouse and the Air Force Entertainment Liaison Board. Darrell is a member of the Beverly Hills Bar Association, Los Angeles County Bar Association, American Bar Association, the Black Entertainment and Sports Lawyers Association, the Recording Academy and the Academy of Television Arts and Sciences.

He is also a frequent panelist and guest moderator of discussions relating to both the talent and institutional aspects of entertainment law.